The Role of HR in the Transforming Workplace

Changing technology and the growing demand for workforce intelligence have ushered in a new era of human resource (HR) transformation and have compelled HR professionals to continually ideate, innovate, and adapt. This book covers the changing role of HR in the transformation of workplaces to be successful globally.

With challenges come new opportunities for HR to completely transform. Currently, technology is considered to be an extension of human beings rather than an external component, which makes people less socially connected. Physical, psychological, and financial well-being in this machine-led world is driving the agenda of HR. Individuals with complex business requirements and long-term goals must coexist with the gig economy, flexible workplaces, and changing priorities. This book precisely addresses these issues.

More innovations are needed to create solutions for an ever-growing digital world. This book, therefore, explains how the role of HR executives must be to understand how emerging technologies are affecting company culture, strategy, operational plans, and the hiring of future talent. Crafting a career path for knowledge workers with challenging roles with fulfilling job aspects remains a puzzle.

Keeping people engaged and happier is one of the major challenges that HR professionals experience. Different generations in the workplace with differing styles of learning, communication, and dynamic expectations add to these challenges. HR functions must keep evolving to overcome these challenges to transform the workplace, and it is essential to recognize how HR can act as a strategic business advisor through the effective use of technology. This book provides practical advice in these areas.

In addition, this book helps professionals, researchers, and practitioners understand the way advanced technology and automation are influencing HR practices and processes in the new normal. The topics are designed to capture the most advanced technology-based HR practices for workplace transformations in industry and academia. This book assembles contributions from experts in HR planning, human capital management, business analytics, people analytics, predictive analysis, and automation from across the world, contributing their knowledge to identify the different attributes of the above-mentioned field of study. The book's chapters are designed and organized pragmatically to enhance the reader's experience and interest, reflecting upon a few untouched segments in the HR domain such as HR data privacy, data security, diversity, and inclusion using explainable AI (XAI), blockchain, and metaverse.

The Role of HR in the Transforming Workplace

Challenges, Technology, and Future Directions

Edited by
Anamika Pandey
Simon Grima
Suruchi Pandey
Balamurugan Balusamy

Routledge
Taylor & Francis Group

A PRODUCTIVITY PRESS BOOK

First published 2024
by Routledge
605 Third Avenue, New York, NY 10158

and by Routledge

4 Park Square, Milton Park, Abingdon, Oxon, OX14 4RN

Routledge is an imprint of the Taylor & Francis Group, an informa business

ISBN: 978-1-032-44532-8 (hbk)
ISBN: 978-1-032-44530-4 (pbk)
ISBN: 978-1-003-37262-2 (ebk)

DOI: 10.4324/9781003372622

Typeset in ITC Garamond
by KnowledgeWorks Global Ltd.

Contents

Foreword vii

Preface ix

Editors xiii

1 Industry 4.0 Inducing Paradigm Changes in Human Resources 1
   POOJA UPADHYAY

2 Robotics in Production and Its Impact on HR Functions 10
   JAGJIT SINGH DHATTERWAL, KULDEEP SINGH KASWAN,
   JYOTI PRAKASH PATHAK, AND BALAMURUGAN BALUSAMY

3 Application of Artificial Intelligence in Human Resource
   Management: A Conceptual Framework 32
   VISHAL SINGH AND AYESHA KHATUN

4 Adoption and Impact of Blockchain Technology on
   Employee Life Cycle 50
   SURUCHI PANDEY AND SANJAY PANDEY

5 Spurring Organisation Performance through Artificial
   Intelligence and Employee Engagement: An Empirical Study 60
   G. P. MISHRA, K. L. MISHRA, S. S. PASUMARTI, D. MUKHERJEE,
   A. PANDE, AND A. PANDA

6 Gig Economy: Changing the Dynamics of the Workforce 79
   MANISHA SURYAWANSHI AND POONAM PONDE

7 Re-Imaging Human Resource Strategic Approaches:
   Adoption of Metaverse 95
   SANKAR MUKHERJEE AND GAURAV GUPTA

8 Blockchain Technology in HR Processes.................................104
KULDEEP SINGH KASWAN, SUMIT KUMAR DHANDA,
JAGJIT SINGH DHATTERWAL, AND BALAMURUGAN BALUSAMY

9 A Study on Value Creation in HR Using Blockchain
Technology...117
BIKRANT KESARI

10 Organizational Factors Affecting Innovative HR Practices
and Systems: A Way to Creating the New Gen Workplace.......129
SUHASINI CHOUDHURY, MAHUYA GHOSH DUTTA,
PADMALITA ROUTRAY, AND ASHOK KUMAR DASH

11 Disengagement to Engagement: A Strategic Employee
Retention Approach with AI...147
SANKAR MUKHERJEE AND POORVI AGRAWAL

12 HR Transformation and Resiliency.......................................156
KASHISH OHRI AND SURUCHI PANDEY

Index 165

Foreword

When Dr. Anamika Pandey requested me to write a foreword for her book, I was taken back 14 years when she joined the Galgotias Business School as a faculty of HR & OB, where I was the director. Her passion for HR was still the same, and so was her determination to excel at everything she did. It is truly my privilege to pen a few thoughts as a "foreword" for a well-edited book *The Role of HR in the Transforming Workplace*, which is comprehensive and insightful, and has the potential to create ripples of change in the HR management profession that are being transformed by new technologies. This new book comes at a time when COVID-19 not only disrupted lives and livelihoods but also caused disruptions in people's practices when companies started leveraging the power of technology to connect and communicate and realized that old HR practices were not sustainable in the face of the rapidly transforming ecosystems and workplace.

This book takes the reader through an existing journey of the disruptive changes in HR functions using AI, social platforms, chatbots, metaverse, robotics, and cloud computing technology for the transformation of workplace. HR professionals must return to the drawing board to create new personalized learning and development using gamification, progressive analytics, and online mentoring. The topic of employee wellness has been addressed as the editors analyze flexible work options. The opportunities opened up by the agile technology-enabled gig economy have been dealt with at length.

This is one of a kind book which the editors have carefully curated wherein details as to how the application of technology has recalibrated the various aspects of the HR functions for developing and transforming the workplaces have been discussed. This book is especially useful for academicians, students, researchers, industry practitioners, and entrepreneurs as its central theme is "people are the initiators as well as the intended beneficiaries" of the technological transformation of the HR function. The editorial team comprising Prof. Balamurugan Balusamy, Prof. Suruchi Pandey, and Prof. Simon Grima is a synergy of people with technical skills and those with vast experience in the field of HR who have equipped the readers with the practical tools and ideas to ride the wave of change.

Prof. (Dr.) Renu Luthra
Advisor to Chancellor and Former Vice-Chancellor
Galgotias University, Greater Noida, India

Preface

Before the pandemic, the most significant disruptions to work were related to new technologies and expanding trade linkages. For the first time, the pandemic has highlighted the relevance of the physical dimension of work. The pandemic compelled businesses and consumers to embrace new behaviors quickly, emphasizing the need for a more dynamic and talented work paradigm. However, it has brought high-level changes that have a profound and immediate impact on how societies operate and how individuals connect and work. The changes have witnessed a large-scale move towards remote work, dynamic resource reallocation, and the rapid growth of digitization and automation to accommodate changing individual and organizational needs. The global economy has also been rattled by these disruptive forces that have altered people's social and professional lives to a more significant extent. Not only did employees' day-to-day work and the tools they used change, but also entire organizational procedures changed.

The automation of complicated tasks has progressed globally quicker than planned. Machines have replaced many tasks, and the few remaining jobs have become more complex, but the supply of competent employees still outweighs the demand. The changing technology and growing demand for workforce intelligence have ushered in a new era of HR transformation and have compelled HR professionals to continually ideate, innovate, and adapt. To be effective and sustainable, HR processes are undergoing a significant transformation in the workplace, especially with many new features coming into play every other day. Rather than just being a simple administrative role, HR today assumes a more strategic role by implementing people-centric objectives and focusing more on creating a more positive work environment. The book covers the changing role of HR in the transformation of workplaces to be successful and sustainable globally.

In HR departments, emerging technologies such as artificial intelligence (AI), Blockchain and Metaverse are frequently used to foster long-term relationships with employees. Technology is also being leveraged at an unprecedented pace to automate routine tasks and enhance data analytics for a better decision-making process. This is also helping in making informed decisions, optimizing and retaining top key talent and identifying key improvement and performance areas. With the world grappling with a pandemic like COVID-19, the adoption of a remote work environment has increased, with the world looking at a healthier work-life balance. This book aims to delve deeper into various nuances of HR in today's workplaces and how they will be transitioning in the future. Right from AI to disruptive technologies, cloud computing technology, the new era of learning and development, improvement in performance and employee well-being, especially in unforeseen circumstances, the gig economy playing a significant role, how employee resiliency helps HR to emerge victorious in challenging situations, innovations being introduced in the field of HR, how blockchain and data validity and creating an impact, and how HR can be made more sustainable in the longer run, the book aims at identifying the current scenarios, challenges, and scope of such topics in the transforming workplace in the present era.

More productivity and more innovations are needed to work solutions for an ever-growing digital world. Therefore, the role of HR executives in the 21st century must be to understand how emerging technologies affect company culture, strategy, operational plans, and the hiring of future talent. Crafting a career path for knowledge workers with challenging roles with fulfilling job aspects remains a puzzle. Keeping people engaged and happier is one of the challenges HR folks experience. Multiple generations at work with various ways of communication, learning, and dynamic expectations add to these challenges. HR functions will have to keep evolving to overcome these challenges to transform the workplace, and it is essential to recognize how HR can act as a strategic business advisor through the effective use of technology. The content of the book highlights the role of disruptive technologies in the growth and sustainability of HR management practices and processes to transform workplaces.

With challenges come new opportunities for HR to transform completely. Nowadays, technology is considered an extension of human beings rather than an external component, making people less socially connected. Physical, psychological, and financial well-being in this machine-led world is driving the agenda of HR. Individuals with complex business requirements and long-term goals must coexist with the gig economy, flexible workplaces, and changing priorities. The book covers a wide range of topics and addresses such issues.

It is increasingly being said that "the role of HR is evolving from traditional administration to driving the employee experience and shaping the culture of the organization." This book will give insights into how the workplace is transforming in actuality, with several dimensions of the workplace being examined today. It shows how HR is embracing agility, enabling automation, adapting to change, and shaping a diverse and inclusive work environment for employees. HR is revolutionizing how we work and thrive in the modern workplace by leveraging technology, focusing on being resilient even in the face of a deadly pandemic like COVID-19 and analyzing data to make informed decisions. Fields like AI, metaverse, and blockchain technology are also being discussed since they help in improving processes like recruitment, background checks, and managing payroll systems along with creating a more equitable and collaborative workforce which aims to enhance efficiency and streamline processes in a better way. The new learning and development trends will also highlight how future trends will amalgamate with technology and make a way into today's learning and development processes and modules. A gig economy today is an evolving landscape with the need to look at talent management, the changing nature of jobs, how various skills are a prerequisite for specific job roles, and how the dynamics of work culture are associated with the gig workers. This book will also explore how innovative trends will take over the marketplace scenario with the new generation adopting various recent trends in every field and what challenges organizations will have to overcome while adopting a more technology-driven front in the workplace. Overall, this book culminates into dimensions which can be researched further and how the workplace will transform and transition for the better for the employees and enhance productivity in the longer run.

Editors

Prof. Anamika Pandey received her DPhil degree in organization from the University of Allahabad, India, in 2011. She is Professor and Associate Dean in the School of Business, Galgotias University, Delhi-NCR, India. Her areas of specialization are HR development, organizational change & development, and technological innovation. She has more than 17 years of academic and industry experiences. Her bachelor's, master's, and DPhil degrees are from the Central University of India. She has more than 15 research papers in high-indexed journals in the area of organizational assessment and techniques, assessment of intangible assets, and stress management. She has also authored two books in the area of HR and technology. In addition to the academic experience, she has also conducted more than 30 management development programs for the armed forces, banking, and manufacturing sectors. She has led many workshops, organized international conferences, and is a member of editorial board of management journals listed in UGC care.

Prof. Simon Grima is the Head of the Insurance Department, in charge of the Bachelor of Commerce in Insurance, the Bachelor of Commerce (Honors) and Master's degree in Insurance and Risk Management, and Associate Professor at the University of Malta. He served as the President of the Malta Association of Risk Management (MARM) and President of the Malta Association of Compliance Officers (MACO) between 2013 and

2015 and between 2016 and 2018, respectively. Moreover, he is among the first Certified Risk Management Professional (FERMA), is the chairman of the Scientific Education Committee of PRIMO, and a member of the curriculum development team of PRIMIA in 2014. His research focus and consultancy is on governance, regulations, and internal controls (i.e., risk management, internal audit, and compliance) and has over 30 years of experience that varies between financial services and public entities in academia, internal controls, investments, and IT. He acts as an Independent Director for financial services firms, sits on Risk, Compliance, Procurement, Investment, and Audit Committees, and carries out duties as a Compliance Officer, Internal Auditor, and Risk Manager. He has acted as co-chair and a member of the scientific program committee on international conferences, and is a chief editor, editor, and review editor of some journals and book series. He was chair of the FERMA awards in 2019 and a mentor for the first FERMA Risk Management Advanced Certification. He has been awarded outstanding reviewer for *Journal of Financial Regulation and Compliance* in the 2017 Emerald Literati Awards.

Dr. Suruchi Pandey is Professor, Symbiosis Institute of Management Studies, Symbiosis International (Deemed) University, Pune, India. Her qualifications include a PhD in management, master's in commerce and management, a diploma in T&D, ADCA, PGDPC, MDHEA, UGC NET, and ACTP certification for ICF. Her areas of interest include HR management, leadership development, inclusion & diversity, and the future role of HR management. She has over two decades of experience in academia and quite a few years in the industry. She has been involved in academic and admission administration. She is a Board of Studies member of Symbiosis International University, Pune, Maharashtra, India, and at the Department of Management, Rajarambapu Institute of Technology, Islampur, Maharashtra, India. She has been nominated as a standing committee member at VAMNICON for faculty evaluation.

She takes keen interest in interdisciplinary research. She has worked on various projects associated with corporations and academia. She has published several papers in international and peer-reviewed journals. She has conducted a number of MDPS and training sessions for corporates. She has three patents registered in India. She is recognized by Skill India

Initiative. She is the recipient of various awards, including Excellence for Teaching by Lexicon Group of Institutes 2023, IRDP Award 2019, Dr. Dewang Mehta Award of Best Faculty in HRM 2013, MCCIA Live Project Competition First Prize and Award, Best Paper Award for HR Track at SIMSARC 2018, and Best Case Study in HRM Award at IBS 2016.

 **Balamurugan Balusamy** is currently working as Associate Dean Student in Shiv Nadar University, Delhi-NCR. Prior to this assignment, he was Professor, School of Computing Sciences & Engineering and Director, International Relations at Galgotias University, Greater Noida, India. His contributions focus on engineering education, blockchain, and data sciences. His academic degrees and 12 years of experience working as a faculty in a global university like VIT University, Vellore, India, has made him more receptive and prominent in his domain. He has 200+ high impact factor papers published with Springer, Elsevier, and IEEE. He has contributed to more than 80 edited and authored books and collaborated with eminent professors across the world from top QS-ranked universities. Dr. Balusamy has served up to the position of Associate Professor in his stint of 12 years of experience with VIT University, Vellore. He completed his bachelor's, master's, and PhD degrees in top premier institutions in India. His passion is teaching and he adapts different design thinking principles while delivering his lectures. He has published 80+ books on various technologies and visited 15+ countries for his technical course. His résumé has several top-notch conference publications and over 200 publications in high-indexed journals, including articles, conference papers, and book chapters. He serves in the advisory committee for several startups and forums and does consultancy work for industry on Industrial IOT. He has given over 195 talks in various events and symposiums.

Chapter 1

Industry 4.0 Inducing Paradigm Changes in Human Resources

Pooja Upadhyay
AISSMS Institute of Management, Pune, India

1.1 Introduction

Human resources (HR) has radically transformed its work processes over the past two decades. Emerging technology has led to the automation of HR processes. It has resulted in an efficient and leaner HR structure. Integrating HR processes with technology was going on slowly pre-COVID. The bouts of COVID have induced high HR integration with technology. HR processes and the economy were put forward to be abreast of digitisation, which led to a massive transformation in HR processes, from e-recruitment, virtual offer letters to virtual training.

Change is an inevitable ongoing process that impacts almost everything everywhere. This constant change has led to the rise of a new digital industrial technology known as 4.0. It can be described as the fourth industrial revolution.

As water and steam were the main components of the first revolution, the second revolution involved mass production in mechanical processes, followed by the implementation of computerised machines in the third revolution. Now we have its extension involving artificial intelligence (AI) and automated machines. As mentioned earlier, this is a stage that we have

DOI: 10.4324/9781003372622-1

reached through steady, continuous developments over the centuries, and this shall not stop here but continue in the same manner we have arrived here.

The First Industrial Revolution can be considered the start, thanks to the arrival of steam machines, water and steam power usage and all other machines. The advent of such machines included trains and the mechanisation of manufacturing.

The Second Industrial Revolution was when electricity and new manufacturing inventions took centre stage. Inventions like assembly line manufacturing and mass production were this era's leading lights, including the introduction of automation.

The Third Industrial Revolution was all about computers, computer networks, the Internet, intranet and robotics in manufacturing and connectivity. Evolutions of e-versions of all processes with a lot of automation were significant achievements.

The Fourth Industrial Revolution is seen as the period where we move very vigorously towards the bridging of digital and cyber-physical systems, the convergence of information technology and operational technology and all other vital technologies such as Big data, high-data transfer, Internet of Things (IoTs) and cloud computing. Additional accelerators such as AI and robotics with complete automation and optimisation will achieve full decentralised control over the final product, which will help to provide ample opportunities and take the industry ahead.

1.2 Importance of Industry 4.0

Industry 4.0 has been defined as the ongoing trend of automation and data exchange in production processes involving cyber-physical systems, robots, cloud computing, IoTs, Industrial Internet of Things, AI and remote servers in creating a complete intelligent manufacturing unit.

Mentioned below are some of the many characteristics of this process:

a. The control previously in the central systems is now distributed in almost all the stages of production.
b. The automation and control are enhanced compared to previous versions.
c. IoTs enable smooth interaction between physical and digital systems.

d. Due to control over every section of manufacturing, customisation and personalisation of products are possible and easy.
e. Because of the communication between the machines, raw materials and power wastage are minimised, resulting in profitable manufacturing.
f. Large amounts of data transfer between machines are possible, leading to immediate change or modification in the component.

To understand the whole concept more straightforwardly, suppose we have many units that function together or are related to the performance of one another. Through the automation and involvement of mechatronics, we had a seamless production. Still, any problem or malfunction at any stage would have to be found out, searched for and fixed, but only after there was a wastage of raw materials, time and power. But now, after the arrival of cyber-physical elements and the IoTs, these machines can relate to each other and communicate their progress from time to time. Any malfunction at any stage is transmitted efficiently, and the process is altered, halted or aborted accordingly. Communication about something going wrong shortly in one of the stages is also possible. This efficient process has affected almost all manufacturing units and operations as well. The vast data transfer and data management allow immediate change at nearly every stage of the process, enhancing the customisation of the final product.

The impact of Industry 4.0 goes far beyond the manufacturing units. This impacts almost all business units involved with design, production, development, transportation, sale of products and logistics. Hence, managers have to know about this and be ready for the challenges and opportunities incorporated with this rapid advancement of Industry 4.0.

HR departments have been increasingly using technology and automation to streamline their processes and improve efficiency. Here are some current practices that HR departments have adopted to enhance automation:

1. **Applicant tracking systems (ATS):** An ATS is a software application that automates recruitment. It can scan resumes, filter applications and schedule interviews, reducing the time and effort required to find and hire the right candidate.
2. **Employee self-service (ESS):** ESS allows employees to access and update their personal information, view their pay stubs and benefits and request time off through an online portal, which reduces the

workload for HR and increases employee satisfaction by providing convenient and easy access to critical information.

3. **Performance management software:** Performance management software automates performance reviews by providing a centralised platform for managers and employees to set goals, track progress and give feedback. This system helps to ensure that performance evaluations are fair, consistent and objective.

4. **Learning management systems (LMS):** An LMS is a software application that automates employee training and development activities. It can deliver online training courses, track employee progress and generate reports on training completion. This makes it easier for HR to manage employee development programs and ensure that employees have the necessary skills and knowledge to perform their jobs effectively.

5. **Chatbots:** Chatbots are computer programs that use AI to simulate conversations with human users. HR departments can use chatbots to automate everyday tasks such as answering frequently asked questions, providing information on benefits and policies and scheduling interviews.

These recent HR automation practices aim to improve efficiency, reduce costs and increase employee satisfaction. By automating routine tasks, HR can focus on more strategic initiatives and provide better support to the organisation.

Some of the significant future changes concerning management and HR constitute:

a. **Enhanced usage of robotics**: Extensive use of robotics, including non-humanoid land robots, aerial drones and stationary robots, is expected in the coming future.

b. **Increased net of technology adaption**: Due to market demands, companies will increase their use of cloud computing, machine learning, the IoTs, augmented reality and virtual reality.

c. **Shifting of employment types**: An increase in remote work arrangements, flex timing work and the inclusion of independent contractors are expected, and there will be a reduction in the full-time workforce.

d. **Enhanced machine work time**: It is foreseen that soon, the machines will be performing increased task hours. Human–machine interaction will focus more on letting machines handle automated jobs, and humans will take on more complex work.

e. **Overall positive job outlook**: There may be some shrinkage in jobs with old skill sets, but there may be good growth in the other profiles.

f. **Various other roles in emergence**: Depending upon the organisation, the required functions will also take on new shapes with the necessary skill sets.

g. **Continuous enhancing skills**: In this scenario, there would always be a requirement for upgrading the capabilities and skill sets according to new technological developments.

h. **Surge in E-commerce**: There would be a sudden surge in the e-commerce sector business and an enhanced dependence on cloud services.

The target and vision are to achieve or enable autonomous self-decision-making processes, monitor them in real time and allow well-connected value-creation networks and horizontal and vertical integration.

Finally, with the addition of efforts towards innovation and transformation of processes, its business enhances the customer experience, decreases costs, optimises customer lifetime value, sells more, grows fast and remains profitable.

1.3 Restructuring Human Resource Strategies Concerning Technological Advancement

HR has to play a vital role as a connector and collaborator so that all technological changes are incorporated and implemented well, which will further help the business produce more value.

According to the McKinsey Global Institute report (2018), by 2030, 375 million workers, or roughly 14% of the global workforce, may need to switch occupational categories as automation, digitisation and advances in AI disrupt the world of work.

The present era is narrowing the gap between people and technology, inducing the physical, digital and biological worlds. The result of this will have an impact on industries, economies and societies (Figure 1.1).

Figure 1.1 Factors to build a robust system of technological advancement. (Authors Representation.)

The HR of the organisation should tactfully handle the workforce transitions. The following steps can be undertaken to build a robust system of technological progress:

1. **Building new leadership capabilities:** HR leaders must play a critical role in preparing companies to successfully adopt and deploy new technologies by guiding, coaching and mentoring the employees for their roles, tasks and skills. The program champions should be identified and trained well to take the baton ahead.
2. **Building change readiness:** As we know, nothing is permanent except change. Each individual should be introduced to an accepting mechanism of change rather than the defensive mechanism of evolution. Changing for the better leads to an enhancement of the sustainability index. Change readiness can be built by organising various awareness programs.
3. **Emphasis on technological integration:** The program champions will act as connectors for the optimal combination of the human workforce and technological automation to ensure a conducive workplace environment for technology integration.
4. **Human capital value mapping:** This technology-induced area is marked by the use of various technical tools to map human efforts

in different domains. These tools will also help to make the system more efficient and effective. For example, if the HRP mapping tool shows overstaffing, which in turn is pulling down the efficiency of the department, a leaner HR department should be proposed, which will lead to faster and more efficient HR operations.

5. **Revamping HR practices:** Learning and relearning new ways of doing things smartly is essential. The highlight of Industry 4.0 is embedding technology in all aspects. The dynamism of business makes things obsolete with time, let it be products or services. Thus, traditional recruiting methods, conventional compensation structuring, etc., should be discarded, and technology-integrated processes and systems must be explored. For example, the old traditional ways of annually doing the performance appraisal are overtaken by maintaining instant online performance appraisal diaries.

1.4 Human Resources Intelligence

HR intelligence, or human resources intelligence, refers to using data analytics and business intelligence techniques to make strategic decisions about HR. Here's an example of HR intelligence in action:

Suppose a company wants to improve employee retention. They could gather data on employee turnover rates, employee satisfaction surveys and performance metrics. They could then use HR intelligence tools to analyse this data and identify trends and patterns that could indicate why employees are leaving.

For example, they might find that employees who don't receive regular feedback or recognition are likelier to leave. With this knowledge, the company can implement programs to give employees more frequent feedback and recognition, which will improve employee satisfaction and reduce employee turnover.

Another example of HR intelligence could be using data to identify skill gaps and training needs within the organisation. By analysing performance data, the company could identify areas where employees are struggling and provide targeted training to help them improve.

Overall, HR intelligence can help organisations make data-driven decisions about their HR, leading to better business outcomes and a more engaged and productive workforce.

HR intelligence, also known as HR intelligence or HR analytics, refers to using data and analytics to make better decisions related to HR management. Here are some examples of HR intelligence:

i. **Predictive hiring analytics:** HR teams can use data and predictive modelling to identify the best candidates for a job. They can analyse factors like job performance, tenure and turnover rates to determine which candidates are most likely to succeed.

ii. **Employee engagement analytics:** HR teams can use surveys and other tools to measure employee engagement and satisfaction. They can then analyse this data to identify trends, determine what factors contribute to high or low concentration and develop strategies to improve engagement.

iii. **Performance management analytics:** HR teams can use data to track employee performance and identify areas for improvement. They can use this information to provide targeted feedback and coaching and to develop individualised performance improvement plans.

iv. **Diversity and inclusion analytics:** HR teams can use data to measure diversity and inclusion metrics, such as representing underrepresented groups within the company. They can use this information to identify areas where diversity and inclusion initiatives are needed and to develop strategies to improve representation.

v. **Succession planning analytics:** HR teams can use data to identify high-potential employees and track their development. This information can be used to develop succession plans, which help ensure that the organisation has the talent it needs to meet its long-term goals.

Furthermore, it can be concluded that integrating HR practices and processes with technology is crucial for the future sustainability of organisations. Here are some reasons why:

a. **Efficiency:** Technology can automate many HR tasks, such as onboarding, payroll processing and benefits administration, which can save time and increase efficiency. This allows HR professionals to focus on more strategic tasks, such as talent management and employee development.

b. **Data-driven decision-making:** Technology can provide real-time data on employee performance, engagement and other metrics for HR teams. This information can be used to make data-driven decisions that lead to better business outcomes.

c. **Employee experience:** Technology can improve the employee experience by providing self-service options for tasks like benefits enrolment and time-off requests. This can increase employee satisfaction and engagement.

d. **Talent acquisition and management:** Technology can help organisations identify and attract top talent and can provide tools for talent development and retention. For example, HR teams can use data analytics and AI to identify high-potential employees and develop personalised development plans.

e. **Compliance:** Technology can help organisations stay compliant with legal and regulatory requirements related to HR. For example, HR software can help ensure that employee data is stored securely and that compliance requirements related to benefits and payroll are met.

In summary, integrating HR practices and processes with technology can help organisations increase efficiency, make better decisions, improve the employee experience, attract and retain top talent and stay compliant with legal and regulatory norms.

References

Gaikwad, H.V., Pardeshi, A.S., & Pandey, S. (2022) Surmounting the Five-Headed Dragon: Best Practices of Technical Institutes in Rural Maharashtra - Success of the Institution in Online Education, In S. Fazzin (Ed), EdTech Economy and the Transformation of Education, IGI Global, pp. 157–167. DOI: 10.4018/978-1-7998-8904-5.ch009

Gaikwad, P., & Pandey, S. (2022) A review on Special Skill Sets from Industry 4.0 Perspective, Proceedings - 2022 2nd International Conference on Electronic and Electrical Engineering and Intelligent System, ICE3IS, 276–281.

Kamble, S., & Pandey, S. (2022) Perception Gap Analysis of "Employability" Amongst Academia, IT-Industry and Fresh Engineering Graduates. ECS Transactions, 107(1), 10857–10864.

McKinsey Global Institute, Retraining and Re-skilling Workers in the Age of Automation, 22nd January 2018.

Chapter 2

Robotics in Production and Its Impact on HR Functions

Jagjit Singh Dhatterwal
Koneru Lakshmaiah Education Foundation, Vaddeswaram, India

Kuldeep Singh Kaswan
Galgotias University, Greater Noida, India

Jyoti Prakash Pathak
Galgotias Institute of Management & Technology, Greater Noida, India

Balamurugan Balusamy
Shiv Nadar University, Greater Noida, India

2.1 Introduction

In the current global and Indian economic systems, robotics is the most fundamental idea. Incorporating technological progress into the company's development as a whole poses formidable challenges to the human element (Abraham et al., 2019). The necessity for robots in an industry may be determined by the company's nature in order to reduce repetitive tasks, manage a vast database, save time, and increase productivity compared to issues involving humans. According to the research, businesses must invest in robotics to reap the long-term benefits of reduced spending on staff pay, benefits, sick days, and other absences. When workers are freed from mundane, repetitive tasks, they can devote more time and energy to

DOI: 10.4324/9781003372622-2

strategic planning, policy execution, and product diversification, all of which are essential to the success of any enterprise, no matter how small (Alcaraz et al., 2012).

2.1.1 The Objective of the Study

- To examine robots' impact on human resources (HR)
- To examine the potential benefits and possible drawbacks of robotic process automation (RPA)
- Intent: To explore RPA in HR settings

2.2 HR Procedure in MNCs

Infosys BPM's research indicates that their customer is a multinational corporation (MNC) engaged in IT, outsourcing, and business. Professional advice to more than a thousand customers in more than 50 countries, the company's staff is dispersed throughout several international locations (Aleksander, 2017). HR manage a wide range of procedures, each comprising several sub-steps that are not only time-consuming but also crucial to the happiness of the company's workers simply because of the expanding size of the consumer base. From an HR standpoint, the most challenging aspect was ensuring that transactions were handled quickly and correctly, that business needs were met, that quality and compliance standards were met, and that workers were happy in Infosys business process managers looked at the client's HR procedures to see where automation and simplification of working with crucial data would be most beneficial (Ancarani et al., 2019). The manual labour was greatly diminished, the pace of production increased, and mistakes were reduced to a negligible level, thanks to automation. Here are a few examples of tasks that become more efficient after being automated.

2.2.1 Background Verification for New Employees

It is time-consuming and labour-intensive to cross-reference employee data like name and date of birth with many databases that include hundreds of thousands of entries. Infosys designed an RPA bot, which, after receiving the necessary database from the published information, does an automated cross-check with the back-end database and generates a process report when the operation has concluded without any human assistance (Andresen & Bergdolt, 2017). On a regular basis, reports are generated and stored in the underlying databases. This extensive procedure was spread over multiple bots to produce the outcome quicker. Prospective candidates have positive perceptions about the same (Pandey & Bahukhandi, 2022).

2.2.2 Generating Appointment Letters to New Joiners

Several processes involved in this procedure must be carried out correctly to ensure accurate written communication. Each worker will need around 15 minutes to finish the job using the manual touch. The study found that RPA decreased the processing time by 90% and spent the whole process without violating any rules or laws about the operation (Dhatterwal & Kaswan, 2021).

2.2.3 Paid-in-Full Employees: A Complete and Final Settlement

This step in the payroll procedure necessitates checking that any outstanding employee payments have been appropriately recorded. Severe problems with compliance and financial loss might result from mistakes in this report. By adhering to the business's RPA deployment, this procedure sped up processing time by 95% and eliminated errors (Bailey et al., 2017).

2.2.4 The Study Found that Infosys BPM's RPA Implementation Brought about the Following Results

With automation, the average amount of human effort needed to complete a job has been reduced by 70%, meaning that humans are no longer necessary. Time spent on intermediate processing and returning requests has decreased by 55% and enhanced precision and error-free work. Infosys BPM's knowledge of RPA has led to significant gains in productivity and accuracy for the client and a compelling business case for expanding automation throughout the client's enterprise (Behrend & Thompson, 2011).

2.3 Robotics

The field of robotics is often referred to as computer devices that intelligently do tasks on behalf of humans. For faster replies and more efficient solutions to corporate challenges, robotics is used to analyse massive databases. However, in many areas of the industry, robots have already surpassed the performance of professionals and human specialists (Bell et al., 2008). While support services like HR and others can adopt this creative method, adoption has been slower so far, even though robot utilisation is at a high level of success in manufacturing. Because businesses have realised the value of investing in the advancement of robotics, the field has expanded rapidly in many different directions. The retail, manufacturing, logistics, and supply chain industries have grown significantly recently (Kaswan et al., 2021).

The goal of robotics research and development is to create robots that can act and move similarly to humans. Robotics encompasses numerous disciplines, including artificial intelligence (AI), machine learning (ML), Electrical Engineering (EE), neural technologies (NT), and others. While there is a lot of pessimism about the impact robots will have on jobs and the economy, there is also a lot of hope for the educational and vocational possibilities robots may provide for businesses and their employees (Bondarouk & Brewster, 2016). Therefore, attempts to study robotic technologies may be broken down into three broad classes: those aimed at replacing human work, facilitating cooperation between humans and machines, and providing new educational possibilities. According to studies of these technologies, there will be a dramatic reduction in the labour force due to automation and robots. Welders, painters, assemblers, and individuals with a lesser degree of education, knowledge, and competency are particularly vulnerable to automation-induced job loss (Bondarouk et al., 2017a).

Humanoid robots may one day replace people in customer-facing professions, such as robot waiters in eateries or automated assistants that guide customers through a company's website. Other studies have demonstrated that robots may significantly impact HRM and, more specifically, unemployment rates in the future. Predictions of widespread job loss and replacement by robots are unlikely to come true due to how socioeconomic and managerial stresses influence AI, digitalisation, and robotic technology. Jobs that demand high degrees of social intelligence, originality, or empathy are less likely to be automated or replaced shortly (Bondarouk et al., 2017b). Many experts in human resource management (HRM) now stress the importance of integrating human skills with technological advances in robotics to develop more sophisticated HR solutions (Pandey & Khaskel, 2019). The future workforce must be better equipped to take advantage of possibilities and protect against risks in the human and robot cohabitation and cooperation era. Human workers could benefit from robots if promoted to higher-level technical roles. The employment of surgical robots is one such application. While automation can potentially increase precision and decrease error rates, it cannot replace human knowledge. In addition to the technical capabilities of healthcare equipment, the doctor's interventions and expertise are often crucial (Kaswan & Dhatterwal, 2021).

HRM students now have access to many new learning opportunities made possible by the rise of robotic technology. Robotics is the study of how machines can do routine jobs currently performed by people, making employees more productive by allowing them to devote their time to more challenging endeavours. However, assisting employees in adjusting to their new positions and acquiring the skills essential to deal with robots opens up new avenues for education in combination with intensive training. However, opinions on robots among employees may differ depending on the nature of the position. The research indicates that high-skilled professionals are more optimistic about robots and their usage because they perceive robotics as a method to further their careers. The future of AI and robotics-based occupations remains to be determined. However, if we use these tools, we might discover approaches to problem-solving that prove pretty useful (Dhatterwal et al., 2022).

2.4 Robotics in HR

Human resource automation's potential to reduce staffing numbers via superior technology is often questioned. Many HR transactional operations can be automated with the right technology. Businesses can save time and resources by automating rule-based, repetitive, and standardised HR tasks (Chang & Smale, 2013). This allows HR professionals to focus on policy development, talent cultivation, and employee retention.

Deloitte (2017) found that 42% of their Global Human Capital Trends survey respondents said that robots had been fully integrated into their workplace or are being introduced gradually. A further poll on global shared services found that 45% of HR professionals anticipate robotics implementation to result in 10% to 20% cost savings for the organisation (Marr, 2015). Due to these trends converging, developers may soon be able to construct software bots to carry out menial tasks (Chao & Kozlowski, 1986).

2.4.1 The Future of Robotics in HR and Business

The development and use of robotics in various manufacturing settings are evidence of the field's rapid growth and expansion. The value of robots may be increased by looking at the digitalised sector from a different angle (Christofi et al., 2019).

2.4.2 Safe and Simple to Implement

RPA is an easy-to-implement, low-risk, non-intrusive technology that may be used with most preexisting infrastructures. Employees benefit from this since it sets the groundwork for ever-expanding machine-learning technologies (Christofi et al., 2017).

2.4.3 Increased Efficiency

By reducing the amount of labour required, RPA may free up staff to concentrate on other high-value job activities more creatively, which can help an organisation achieve its objectives by enhancing its overall effectiveness (Colbert et al., 2016).

2.4.4 Cost

Compared to other operational sources, RPA's cost is negligible and might vary widely depending on the organisation's requirements. Unlike other investments, RPA requires a single payment over a longer time frame.

2.4.5 Accuracy

Data analysis is one area where RPA excels at human efficiency levels, producing accurate and exact results.

2.4.6 Productive Work

Many manufacturers use RPA to speed up and simplify their assembly lines. This robot can do high-quality work with more precision and accuracy. They can work non-stop if they have electricity, and their work is guaranteed higher quality and more error-free than human employees (Dhatterwal et al., 2023b).

2.4.7 *Implementing Lean Process*

The use of robotics greatly aids lean manufacturing. When inefficient procedures are eliminated, a company is more efficient and productive. This approach focuses on adjusting processes and procedures to meet the needs of consumers better. Their pinpoint precision also helps cut down on material waste. Robowork's return on investment (ROI)is so high because it cuts costs immediately during manufacturing (ROI) (Cooke et al., 2017). Expenses for both upkeep and set-up are rising. Small and medium-sized businesses may be unable to afford the growth of robots, but some firms launch the software with little cost. Incorporating robots into the workplace might be too expensive for certain businesses. Employers and owners should exercise caution when investing in this because of the upfront and ongoing costs involved in the system's purchase, installation, and upkeep (Cooke et al., 2019).

2.4.8 *Loss of Jobs and Reduced Opportunities*

The resulting societal problem of mass joblessness caused by increasing mechanisation is a genuine concern. With the proliferation of more sophisticated technologies, the pool of available human specialists will shrink as the importance of robots in the workplace increases. Medical diagnosticians and surgeons aren't immune to the potential layoffs caused by the widespread use of workplace automation (Dhatterwal & Baliyan, 2023).

2.5 Digitalisation in HR

Numerous HR procedures might be brought into the current day by the use of AI. AI in the HR department may take several forms, including recruitment, applicant screening, interview scheduling, and profile matching. "HR executives need to experiment with all the dimensions of AI to offer value to their firm," says Jeanne Meister, according to Forbes articles. This is raising issues pertaining to reskilling jobs (Kamble & Pandey, 2022).

2.5.1 *Coding*

All the articles that may be helpful for this research were saved. Reading each article via a filter collected the data we needed for a data extraction form. Doing so helps remove the possibility of human mistakes while documenting the process so that interested parties may repeat and see it. Publication information, paper type (empirical, conceptual, and review), and our standardising review's anticipated results (De Kock et al., 2020) required that all relevant definitions, units of analysis, effects of automated procedures on HRM, essential outcomes, and subsequent areas of examination provided by the authors of each study be encoded and loaded into a spreadsheet created with Excel.

2.5.2 Thematic Analysis

Academic research on technology-enabled examined publications covers a wide range of themes and situations since HRM has studied so many different things. The purpose of this section was to highlight the most important results from the research. To answer our research questions, we looked for shared characteristics among articles, which we then used to group into research themes organised by the unit of analysis. There were found to be three primary areas of study: (1) cutting-edge technology, (2) AI, and (3) robots. We organised the papers by these three categories of analysis. In Section 2.5.3, entitled "Advanced Technologies," 16 essays were compiled to discuss how IT and related technological advancements have begun to impact HRM. The second subject accounts for the bulk of the articles, which focus on the effects of AI on topics including job elimination, collaboration, education, deliberation, and staffing involving AI and humans. Seven papers under the third subject (robotics) attempt to make sense of robots' influence on HRM and working environments, particularly in job substitution, human-robot cooperation, and the development of new educational possibilities. Consistent with other state-of-the-art systematic reviews, we do not perform a meta-analysis of every single study but instead highlight the most salient findings. It gives a synopsis of the reviewed literature, organised according to the study's three overarching themes (Dhatterwal et al., 2023a).

2.5.3 Advanced Technologies

The proliferation of IT has caused changes in organisational structures, policies, and roles. Therefore, academics are increasingly interested in electronic human resource management (eHRM) (the intersection of IT and HRM) to understand better the external rather than internal impacts on business operations and HRM. These developments are affecting HRM generally, not only in HRM jargon. The result has been rethinking company policies around employee management and the launch of ground-breaking new goods and services. It outlines five affordances resulting from this interaction, such as the ability to see the whole process from start to finish, to be more agile and creative when developing new products and services, to work together virtually, to work in a large group, to engage in simulation and synthetic reality, and so on (Dulebohn & Hoch, 2017).

Electronic recruitment, sometimes known as "e-recruitment," has been the topic of much academic discourse. According to the available literature, there are several advantages of automatically correlating job offers with appropriate profiles of candidates, including decreased effort (in terms of cost and time), elimination of the need for HR managers to have knowledge alluding to a particular area of expertise or speciality, and an increase in positive applicant perceptions of the company. The use of the Internet in recruitment—known as "e-recruitment"—has profoundly impacted the labour market.

A massive body of work details how computers and other forms of cutting-edge technology have changed HRM. IoT's application in HRM necessitates adjustments to the hardware, software, and data used in HR, as well as HR activities (such as permitting more flexible work hours, increasing productivity among staff, and personalising their office space) and HR personnel (tasks and qualifications). With the help of employee self-service (ESS) software, workers may see and change their personal information and sign up for training without contacting the HR department. Electronic performance measurement (EPM) might have far-reaching effects on HR, especially in the evaluation, recruitment, and promotion processes. In addition to the various forms of EPM currently in use (such as call and Internet usage monitoring and electronic medication administration records), technologies such as microchip wrist implantation and body heat sensor desk hardware may represent the future of work surveillance. In addition to helping employees, companies may utilise algorithmic technology for coaching, evaluation, and discipline. Particularly, fascinating in the realm of virtualisation today are technologies that enable the modelling of human interaction in digital, three-dimensional situations. Although these tools were initially developed for use in the gaming industry, they now find widespread application in the business world, helping employees better collaborate and share information (Edwards, 1954).

The data needs to be more balanced when it comes to whether or not HRM facilitated by technology offers substantial strategic benefits. New security threats have emerged due to developments in information technology and other forms of innovative technology, along with benefits (cost savings, harmonisation and integration of HR processes, efficiency, and support for global strategy). Researchers have theorised that an event's meaning is heavily influenced by its context. Variables such as company size, industry, and geography might mitigate the impact of technology-enabled HRM on certain businesses. It's possible to see it as risky but many believe it's essential in today's economy.

Employee repercussions are still unknown. There will be a net gain in employment, but the nature of the new positions will shift. Since problem-solving and interpersonal communication are difficult for robots to mimic, a new set of skills will be necessary. It predicts that as full-time jobs become less common, more individuals seek freelance and part-time opportunities. There is a danger that stakeholders have become even more distant due to HRM developments, which have helped break down geographical barriers. Although HR technology has many benefits, this essay argues that it should be used as a decision-support tool that complements existing human resource professionals rather than replacing them.

2.5.4 Intelligence Synthesised

"Artificial intelligence" in the context of computers refers to systems that, although not acting identically to people, may nonetheless simulate intelligent activities. Machine learning and deep neural networks are two branches of AI that have attracted attention from academics across domains due to their numerous practical applications. Job replacement, human-AI interaction, training, decision-making, and recruitment are all directly related to the study of AI, creating a direct link between HRM and AI research.

Considering the potential services that AI may one day provide is a good starting point for understanding the HRM challenges posed by AI. One argument along these lines holds that "lower" intellectual jobs will be mechanised first since they are more straightforward and require less time on a computer.

Human work will be replaced by AI that can mimic human thought and emotion. Consequently, people will need time to feel comfortable opening out to one another. Consider Siri and other virtual assistants seriously. They need to set up shops in various parts of the world to answer queries from customers anywhere in the world. It argues that unskilled people in developed countries may become jobless and "unemployable" (Feldman & Klaas, 2002) because of the rapid development of AI, automation, and digitalisation.

In light of the above, we conclude that progress in AI represents a grave threat to the future of human work. However, the current state of human-machine interaction and integration leaves much to be desired. Professionals in the field believe AI can significantly improve customer service and sales interactions. Particularly, machine learning trained on data gleaned from FLE-client interactions may aid in processing interaction-based knowledge, investigating variability between encounters, and clarifying ambiguous patterns. This paves the way for FLEs to use the information to provide individualised services to their clientele. Artificially intelligent (AI) devices, such as those that can learn on the fly and understand natural language, can improve human relationships and solve problems. The use of AI algorithms in the field of reporting can benefit professionals in crucial roles beyond the scope of their original programming, freeing up journalists to focus on investigative work while increasing the efficiency, scale, and accuracy of news production. In addition, AI (typically in Personal Digital Assistance) may allow workers to do their tasks from anywhere. In sum, these findings bolster the case that automation technology's impact on staffing choices is very contextual and only sometimes results in fewer employment prospects if a facility is strategically located within its local market.

Essential components of AI include the ability to analyse data, reason abstractly, and perform computational tasks. Employees may benefit from opportunities to learn and grow to acquire these sophisticated abilities. AI solutions may be helpful in HRM when implemented in conventional academic institutions. AI settings or simulations have the potential for extensive social interaction between users and improved educational prospects. The cost of simulation-based programs is higher, but they provide a valuable learning opportunity for workers by letting them see the effects of their decisions on the environment and the performance of many rivals. AI character animations have also been examined for their potential as training aids; these characters might provide feedback and help like genuine trainers. The problems of poor interest and confinement in web-based training may be solvable using intelligent computers that can learn in real-time and customise training to workers' claims and external sources. Researchers have been pondering this same subject to understand how AI computer agents may be used to improve humans' strategic and negotiating abilities.

There has been a flurry of new studies analysing the advantages, disadvantages, and risks that recent developments in AI have posed to traditional HRM decision-making. Research into the use of AI as a decision-making tool in HRM has shown that expert systems, which are

AI applications that embody the knowledge and decision-making abilities of a human expert, improve the accuracy of managerial choices made by non-experts while decreasing the time spent making such decisions. AI expert systems may be of tremendous assistance to managers because, first, they facilitate decision-making and, second, they provide light on the rationale behind a specific course of action. Studies that use AI in HRM decision-making show the effectiveness of the technology in evaluating enormous volumes of data, its capacity to aid salespeople in acquiring new clients, and its feasibility in accurately assessing and managing the risk of employee turnover. Human resources management (HRM) decision-making involving AI is likely to be viewed as a threat to human staff members' autonomy, status, and job security because it can provide additional options and confound them, causing advancement in perception. Both human leaders and AI systems may benefit from adopting more equitable procedures, as pointed out by Opting and Maier.

In addition, AI might be utilised to create a testing and hiring setting that is so lifelike it would be impossible to fail. To begin, HRM AI software has made it easier to check references and determine salaries for various positions. AI-based recruiting systems are more objective and unbiased than humans, and they can predict candidates' actions regarding their potential performance and fit with the organisation. Machine learning may be of great use to healthcare professionals and companies by making the selection process more organised by eliminating the chance of recruiter biases or even applicants influencing ways to diverge from the selection method. AI's significant advancements in the HRM recruitment process are certainly progress. However, the effects' widespread appeal among candidates and questions about the ethics of data collection and advancement may nullify some of the positive findings. Legitimate privacy and ethical problems are raised by using AI machine learning and deep learning in HR management. There are serious privacy problems with the direct uses of AI machine learning in the job and HR sector, such as using digital data to supplement conventional psychological testing in assessing talent and forecasting work-related difficulties. Digital interviews with deep AI learning to record and manipulate verbal and non-verbal behaviour to generate a personality profile and forecast compatibility have similar privacy issues.

Based on the discussion mentioned earlier and our analysis of cutting-edge technologies, we have concluded that the HRM industry is now transitioning from the e-HRM era into a new one characterised by the growing role of AI. Recruiting, training, and decision-making are just a few of the HRM fields where intelligent automation is used. We should recognise that AI has a voice in the future of HRM even though many unexplored avenues and obstacles must be overcome (Ferraris et al., 2019).

2.6 HRM Framework Development

The impact of automated thinking on HR management is shown graphically in Figure 2.1 as a potential organisational structure created from the topic analysis. This conceptual framework suggests that AI, robotics, and other state-of-the-art technology might be used to implement intelligent automation in HR administration. HRM increasingly makes use of these methods, which in turn alter the techniques of attracting, educating, and work efficiency; change the practices for making decisions of enterprises; increase the possibility of job replacement; facilitate interaction among robots and AI technology and employees; and provide staff members with options for learning. The model also underlines the HRM intelligent automation consequences for enterprises and employees.

AI, robotics, and other cutting-edge technology may one day help HR departments. HR actions and initiatives are considered as a model capable of mapping the impact of these technologies across levels. Tasks in HR include recruiting, interviewing candidates, providing training, and assessing employee performance. HRM solutions address human-robot/AI collaboration, decision-making, and education/training issues by establishing objectives and implementing HRM procedures. When taken together, these considerations provide a picture of intelligent automation's potential influence on future productivity in the workplace and business.

The actual effects of intelligent automation within HRM settings, whether positive or negative, are mapped out in the current study. The repercussions might be felt on a personal or a societal scale. The effects of technology on the character of work, such as shifts in responsibilities and skillsets required,

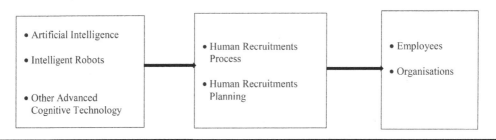

Figure 2.1 Organisational structure framework.

as well as the impact on workers' health and happiness, are examples of the consequences at the individual level. Organisational repercussions may be organised into operational and transformational categories using previous research. Positive effects on productivity and efficiency are highlighted due to operational factors. The repercussions will have a far-reaching impact, particularly on the way businesses operate and the models they use.

This systematic review's suggested integrative framework serves as a guide for future studies and aids in categorising and formulating existing findings. It is hoped that this paradigm will be used as a jumping-off point for other studies that examine the implications of various technologies on HRM and, in turn, the consequences these technologies have on individual workers and their companies. Finally, this paradigm provides valuable insights for managers by connecting academic research to the circumstances they face in the workplace.

2.7 Intelligent Automation in the HR Field

The primary goal of this research was to examine the current literature on intelligent automation in HRM contexts and identify the most serious problems and their implications for HR strategy and practice. We found 45 papers in scholarly journals that, when combined, summed up the state of the art in this field. Some of the problems encountered in those studies could be solved by improving HRM. Compared to other technological fixes or, more recently, big data, the analysis of AI and intelligent automation has lagged. The theoretical ramifications should be emphasised, notwithstanding the topic's freshness and the absence of a well-developed understanding of AI's role in the working world.

We discovered that by expanding on the concept of decision-making and drawing from previous studies that examined how data enables HR managers to get a deeper understanding of people, AI algorithms and expert systems enhance HR processes and facilitate better decision-making concerning human workers and HR practices. Thanks to this, those who need to be better versed in HRM will be able to make better decisions. Therefore, AI is crucial for strengthening the validity of HR evaluations.

Our chapter shows that HRM's use of cutting-edge technologies and AI-driven tools spans various academic disciplines. For this reason, we emphasise the need for scholars drawing from several fields to comprehend it properly. To better understand the ethical challenges posed by AI technologies in decision-making procedures and the factors determining the degree to which human employees are willing to embrace these technologies, academics in HR and information management (IM) or computer engineers could work together.

■ This study explores how AI, robots, and other advanced technologies could modify HRM procedures and their effects on businesses and employees. Our research shows that there is still some time to go before we see the widespread impact on HRM and employment numbers, despite earlier forecasts.
■ There are many moving parts in cutting-edge technologies such as AI, robots, and others, and they need to consider possible difficulties and dangers. Because the topic is so new that it raises serious technical and ethical challenges, several writers have offered valuable ideas that are likely to be implemented gradually as the usage of AI and related technologies grows. Data security is one area where a dispute resolution approach based on efficiency, equality, and voice helps reconcile the sometimes divergent goals of workers and employers functioning on a regional and global scale.

In conclusion, the methodology used in our research has merit. While other literature reviews on e-HRM or big data exist, this one is the most comprehensive because it employs a systematic review methodology to examine every facet of HR management. Including journal papers from various academic fields significantly improves our study's quality. We present a map of the several research sub-areas on this problem across disciplines, elaborating their preliminary results and crucial ideas. Lastly, this research contributes to our understanding of the processes and conditions under which technological developments may result in specific outcomes by providing a framework for future academics to analyse the many roles that technology may play in HRM (Fleming, 2019).

2.8 Managerial Implications in HRM

Due to the novelty of intelligent automation as a field of HRM research, the findings of this extensive literature review are theoretically and practically intriguing and consequential. This research contributes to the growing body of literature arguing that corporate decision-makers should prioritise the favourable benefits of modern technologies on productivity. AI technology improves human employees' social connections, problem-solving efficiency, training, feedback, and general support. That's why companies must foster an environment conducive to collaboration between people and robots. Further, our findings suggest that companies should invest in training and ongoing professional development for their employees to ensure they have the knowledge and expertise to work productively with AI bots. Workers' study habits and abilities may both benefit from training. Thus, managers may encourage their employees to sign up. Managers have a moral duty to equip their employees with the technical literacy training they need to compete in today's global economy.

Consequently, it would be essential to form diverse and flexible relationships with government and public actors, research organisations, and universities to acquire the required technical knowledge. HRM experts would be wise to see technology as a supplemental resource rather than a substitute, even though there are advantages to an HRM strategy that primarily relies on technology. A genuine human brain is required to acquire the relevant knowledge and execute the necessary tasks. Our findings suggest that intelligent automation may increase the effectiveness of HRM, but only if leaders resist the temptation to let technology usurp and supplant HRM's real purpose. Instead, HR pros should focus on enhancing HRM and intelligent technology.

A variety of privacy problems have arisen in HRM due to the proliferation of AI, Machine learning (ML), and Deep learning (DL) applications for the analysis and collection of electronic data in forecasting work-related difficulties. There is a growing need to enact legislation that safeguards the rights of workers or prospective employees to protect data in light of the privacy and ethical concerns associated with this employment. Although the General Data Protection Regulation (EU, 2016/679) is a significant improvement, it will require frequent revisions to keep up with the lightning-fast pace at which technology advances and to educate the public and workers.

Finally, in the context of global HRM, managers should consider how AI technologies reduce the need for travel and personal interaction among all parties involved in digital media. To get there, it will be essential to make it easier for many people to use many technologies to work together on the same project.

2.9 Limitations and Future Research Directions

There are a few caveats to this assessment and you should be aware of them. The review starts on the wrong foot by focusing only on scholarly articles. More research is needed to complement the existing body of work, which could lead to a proliferation of classification schemes. This is because there is the possibility that high-quality material has been published in outlets other than those subjected to peer review. Second, as was previously said, it's possible that we still need to come across any crucial peer-reviewed scientific literature. Third, it's possible that the applied keyword formula concealed the objects of interest.

Further publications focusing on intelligent automation may have yet to be noticed by the search criteria due to the increasing complexity of the HRM architecture due to technological advancements and the substantial interconnection of HRM, GM, IB, and IM problems. The gamut of intelligent automation from an HRM viewpoint is covered in the publications we selected, although this is likely different from a typical sampling. Because there have been so many technological innovations, each of which has been studied using a unique method, it is also challenging to decide which studies to include and which to exclude. However, we are confident that the papers we've chosen represent the vast majority of articles published in top HRM, GM, IB, and IM journals and that this has allowed us to spot a unifying theme.

Therefore, there is inconsistency in the HRM knowledge base, and the question of whether or not eHRM can become a valued strategic partner has not been adequately addressed. It is useful to go back ten years and examine the same problem after noting the scarcity of theory-driven and evidence-based eHRM studies in this still-nascent research area. Uncertainty and potential reward are both high.

As new technologies stretch the limits of business and management, we expect the HRM environment to undergo significant transformation in the following years. For the reasons given below, we have chosen to concentrate our future research lines on the international setting, even though there are many other exciting areas for further exploration. First, we recognise the significance of studying how technology-enabled HRM is employed worldwide and exploring the influence of international factors on HRM implementation. Second, the setting in which a technology is introduced may substantially affect its likelihood of being adopted and used. Third, HRM has been assigned a more significant strategic role as a primary predictor of global corporate performance due to the technological revolution and the rapid speed of internationalisation.

Organisations' HR activity and strategy transfer across borders take time and effort. To determine whether the dynamics encompassing the role of intelligent automation in HR operations and techniques are affected by nation-specific variables or whether a global HRM model can be achieved, it would be helpful to examine how technology-enabled HRM is delivered in different national contexts. For multinationals to succeed, they need to understand why certain HR practices have persisted while others have changed in response to technological developments. More research is required to identify the macro-contextual barriers to the international adoption of automated intelligence in HRM and to investigate possible countermeasures.

Another uncharted territory that may benefit from further study is employees' perspectives on HRM's evolving role in the workplace as a result of technology advancements. Understanding how cultural variations and similarities across national workforces may benefit or impede efforts to apply intelligent automation in HRM is greatly aided by adopting a global viewpoint. Furthermore, it is increasingly likely that robots will replace humans in many occupations. The rise of robots in the workplace will also have consequences for management and upper management. Given the challenges of people management in a global context, it would be instructive to examine the impact of AI on different groups at different tiers of an organisation (Frey & Osborne, 2017).

Present evidence that consumers are open to AI from the consumer's point of view. Therefore, future research could look into how receptive customers are to these advancements and under what conditions AI is most useful for connecting with customers. To accurately measure client approval, it is essential to consider regional variances rather than adopt a worldwide approach. The findings of international comparative research will help future practitioners make worldwide strategic judgements on the displacement of human labour with AI. Consumers' willingness to make sacrifices to embrace new technologies successfully is vital, and the influence of smart technologies on consumer engagement is non-linear, meaning it may move up or down over time. Therefore, gaining a deeper understanding of how AI and robotics have evolved HR practices over time is essential. In conclusion, technology's part in HRM goes beyond aiding and adjusting HR procedures.

The extent to which internationalisation's effects and processes may be applied elsewhere is a hot debate. There is an urgent need for large-scale studies to illustrate how conventional and modern ways of managing personnel may be harmonised for the advantage of all parties since they are the only way to handle this complex and multidisciplinary problem. Our study will pave the way for more investigation into our suggested avenues, the findings of which are crucial for actual application.

2.9.1 Creating Employment Opportunities

Gartner predicted that by 2020, AI will have produced 2.1 million new jobs. This number is based on the estimation that automation has simplified the tasks of 1.8 million jobs. Professionals were urged to enrol in AI programs to be ahead of the curve as technological advances in robots become commonplace. Thus, experts in robotics and AI are needed at all points throughout the product life cycle.

Capgemini found that, out of a sample of 1,000 businesses, 79% used robots in their new positions.

2.9.2 Business Operations and Decision Support

Conferences, team meetings, and business travels are some business activities that benefit from using AI. IBM predicts that by 2025 data-based decision-making tools will be worth $2 trillion and AI will soon be used to help with decision-making.

2.10 Conclusion

In conclusion, the integration of robotics in production is reshaping the role of the HR function within organisations. The rapid advancement of automation and robotics technology presents both challenges and opportunities for HR professionals. The abstract has highlighted the impact of robotics on the workforce, including shifts in job roles, the need for upskilling and reskilling, and potential job displacement. HR plays a critical role in navigating these changes by implementing effective talent management strategies, conducting workforce planning, and facilitating skill development programs to ensure a smooth transition for employees. Moreover, the abstract emphasises the importance of HR in managing human-robot collaboration in the production environment. HR professionals must address training needs, ensure the safety of employees working alongside robots, and facilitate effective communication channels. By fostering a positive work culture and supporting employees during this transition, HR can mitigate resistance to change and promote employee engagement.

In summary, integrating robotics in production requires HR professionals to adapt their strategies to the changing landscape. By embracing the opportunities of automation and robotics, organisations can enhance productivity and efficiency. Simultaneously, HR's role in workforce planning, talent management, and change management is crucial to ensuring a smooth transition and cultivating a supportive and engaged workforce.

References

Abraham, M., Niessen, C., Schnabel, C., Lorek, K., Grimm, V., Moslein, K., & Wrede, M. (2019). Electronic monitoring at work: The role of attitudes, functions, and perceived control for the acceptance of tracking technologies. Human Resource Management Journal, 29(4), 657–675. https://doi.org/10.1111/1748-8583.12250

Alcaraz, J. M., Domenech, M., & Tirado, F. (2012). eHR software, multinational corporations and emerging China: Exploring the role of information through a postcolonial lens. Information and Organization, 22(2), 106–124. https://doi.org/10.1016/j.infoandorg.2012.01.004

Aleksander, I. (2017). Partners of humans: A realistic assessment of the role of robots in the foreseeable future. Journal of Information Technology, 32(1), 1–9. https://doi.org/10.1057/s41265-016-0032-4

Ancarani, A., Di Mauro, C., & Mascali, F. (2019). Backshoring strategy and the adoption of Industry 4.0: Evidence from Europe. Journal of World Business, 54(4), 360–371. https://doi.org/10.1016/j.jwb.2019.04.003

Andresen, M., & Bergdolt, F. (2017). A systematic literature review on the definitions of global mindset and cultural intelligence – merging two different research streams. The International Journal of Human Resource Management, 28(1), 170–195. https://doi.org/10.1080/09585192.2016.1243568

Bailey, C., Madden, A., Alfes, K., & Fletcher, L. (2017). The meaning, antecedents and outcomes of employee engagement: A narrative synthesis. International Journal of Management Reviews, 19(1), 31–53. https://doi.org/10.1111/ijmr.12077

Behrend, T. S., & Thompson, L. F. (2011). Similarity effects in online training: Effects with computerised trainer agents. Computers in Human Behavior, 27(3), 1201–1206. https://doi.org/10.1016/j.chb.2010.12.016

Bell, B. S., Kanar, A. M., & Kozlowski, S. W. (2008). Current issues and future directions in simulation-based training in North America. The International Journal of Human Resource Management, 19(8), 1416–1434. https://doi.org/10.1080/09585190802200173

Bondarouk, T., & Brewster, C. (2016). Conceptualising the future of HRM and technology research. The International Journal of Human Resource Management, 27(21), 2652–2671. https://doi.org/10.1080/09585192.2016.1232296

Bondarouk, T., Harms, R., & Lepak, D. (2017a). Does e-HRM lead to better HRM service? The International Journal of Human Resource Management, 28(9), 1332–1362. https://doi.org/10.1080/09585192.2015.1118139

Bondarouk, T., Parry, E., & Furtmueller, E. (2017b). Electronic HRM: Four decades of research on adoption and consequences. The International Journal of Human Resource Management, 28(1), 98–131. https://doi.org/10.1080/09585192.2016.1245672

Chang, Y. Y., & Smale, A. (2013). Expatriate characteristics and the stickiness of HRM knowledge transfers. The International Journal of Human Resource Management, 24(12), 2394–2410. https://doi.org/10.1080/09585192.2013.781436

Chao, G. T., & Kozlowski, S. W. (1986). Employee perceptions on the implementation of robotic manufacturing technology. Journal of Applied Psychology, 71(1), 70–76. https://doi.org/10.1037/0021-9010.71.1.70

Christofi, M., Leonidou, E., & Vrontis, D. (2017). Marketing research on mergers and acquisitions: A systematic review and future directions. International Marketing Review, 34(5), 629–651. https://doi.org/10.1108/IMR-03-2015-0100

Christofi, M., Vrontis, D., Thrassou, A., & Shams, S. R. (2019). Triggering technological innovation through cross-border mergers and acquisitions: A micro-foundational perspective. Technological Forecasting and Social Change, 146, 148–166. https://doi.org/10.1016/j.techfore.2019.05.026

Colbert, A., Yee, N., & George, G. (2016). The digital workforce and the workplace of the future. Academy of Management Journal, 59(3), 731–739. https://doi.org/10.5465/amj.2016.4003

Cooke, F. L., Veen, A., & Wood, G. (2017). What do we know about cross-country comparative studies in HRM? A critical review of literature in the period of 2000-2014. The International Journal of Human Resource Management, 28(1), 196–233. https://doi.org/10.1080/09585192.2016.1245671

Cooke, F. L., Wood, G., Wang, M., & Veen, A. (2019). How far has international HRM travelled? A systematic review of literature on multinational corporations (2000–2014). Human Resource Management Review, 29(1), 59–75. https://doi.org/10.1016/j.hrmr.2018.05.001

De Kock, F. S., Lievens, F., & Born, M. P. (2020). The profile of the 'Good Judge' in HRM: A systematic review and agenda for future research. Human Resource Management Review, 30(2), 100667. https://doi.org/10.1016/j.hrmr.2018.09.003

Deloitte. (2017). Robots are ready. Are you? Deloitte Consulting Report 2017.

Dhatterwal, J. S., & Baliyan, A. (2023). Digital Flow-Based Cyber-Physical Microfluidic Biochips. In Cyber-Physical Systems (pp. 1–14). Chapman and Hall/CRC.

Dhatterwal, J. S., Baliyan, A., & Prakash, O. (2023a). Reliability Driven and Dynamic Re-Synthesis of Error Recovery in Cyber-Physical Biochips. In Cyber-Physical Systems (pp. 15–34). Chapman and Hall/CRC.

Dhatterwal, J. S., Kaswan, K. S., Jaglan, V., & Vij, A. (2022). Machine Learning and Deep Learning Algorithms for IoD. In The Internet of Drones (pp. 237–292). Apple Academic Press.

Dhatterwal, J. S., Kaswan, K. S., & Kumar, N. (2023b). Telemedicine-Based Development of M-Health Informatics Using AI. In Deep Learning for Healthcare Decision Making (p. 159). CRC Press.

Dhatterwal, J. S., & Kaswan, K. S., & Preety (2021). Intelligent Agent-Based Case Base Reasoning Systems Build Knowledge Representation in COVID-19 Analysis of Recovery of Infectious Patients. In Applications of Artificial Intelligence in COVID-19, Springer (pp. 185–209).

Dulebohn, J. H., & Hoch, J. E. (2017). Virtual teams in organisations. Human Resource Management Review, 27(4), 569–574. https://doi.org/10.1016/j.hrmr.2016.12.004

Edwards, W. (1954). The theory of decision making. Psychological Bulletin, 51(4), 380–417. https://doi.org/10.1037/h0053870

Feldman, D. C., & Klaas, B. S. (2002). Internet job hunting: A field study of applicant experiences with online recruiting. Human Resource Management, 41(2), 175–192. https://doi.org/10.1002/hrm.10030

Ferraris, A., Erhardt, N., & Bresciani, S. (2019). Ambidextrous work in smart city project alliances: Unpacking the role of human resource management systems. The International Journal of Human Resource Management, 30(4), 680–701. https://doi.org/10.1080/09585192.2017.1291530

Fleming, P. (2019). Robots and organisation studies: Why robots might not want to steal your job. Organization Studies, 40(1), 23–38. https://doi.org/10.1177/0170840618765568

Frey, C. B., & Osborne, M. A. (2017). The future of employment: How susceptible are jobs to computerisation? Technological Forecasting and Social Change, 114, 254–280. https://doi.org/10.1016/j.techfore.2016.08.019

Kamble, S., & Pandey, S. (2022). Perception gap analysis of "employability" amongst academia, IT-industry and fresh engineering graduates. ECS Transactions, 107(1), 10857–10864.

Kaswan, K. S., & Dhatterwal, J. S. (2021). The Use of Machine Learning for Sustainable and Resilient Buildings. In Digital Cities Roadmap: IoT-Based Architecture and Sustainable Buildings (pp. 1–62). Springer.

Kaswan, K. S., Dhatterwal, J. S., & Kumar, K. (2021). Blockchain of Internet of Things-Based Earthquake Alarming System in Smart Cities. In Integration and Implementation of the Internet of Things Through Cloud Computing (pp. 272–287). IGI Global.

Marr, B. (2015). Big Data: 20 Mind-Boggling Facts Everyone Must Read *Forbes* Available from: https://www.forbes.com/sites/bernardmarr/2015/09/30/big-data-20-mind-boggling-factseveryone-must-read/#26c704f317b1 [Accessed: 7th April 2018]

Pandey, S., & Bahukhandi, M. (2022). Applicants' perception towards the application of AI in recruitment process. 2022 International Conference on Interdisciplinary Research in Technology and Management, IRTM 2022.

Pandey, S., & Khaskel, P. (2019). Application of AI in human resource management and Gen Y's reaction. International Journal of Recent Technology and Engineering (IJRTE), 8(4), 10325–10331.

Pandey, S., Ruhela, V., & Ruhela, S. (2021). Precursors and ramifications of creativity on innovation in product design teams-a study on Indian information technology sector. Journal of Physics: Conference Series, 1860(1), 012014.

Chapter 3

Application of Artificial Intelligence in Human Resource Management: A Conceptual Framework

Vishal Singh

Lovely Professional University, Phagwara, India

Ayesha Khatun

Symbiosis International University, Nagpur, India

3.1 Introduction

In the current era, terminologies such as artificial intelligence (AI) and machine learning (ML) have garnered evident focus from academicians and industry professionals. AI is a multidisciplinary field that intends to create a replica of human abilities and cognitive behaviour. The widespread adoption of AI technologies results from disruptive innovation enabled by significant improvements in digital infrastructure and the growing interconnection of the world through globalization (Radovic & Badawy, 2020). Recent evidence shows that while global investment in AI tools and technologies has been growing, in India, investment in these areas still needs to be improved in research and practical applications. It has been observed that only a small number of organizations in India are currently utilizing AI technologies (Pandey et al., 2021).

DOI: 10.4324/9781003372622-3

The integration of AI technology in various business processes, including human resources (HR), has the potential to enhance a company's competitiveness. By utilizing AI in HR, organizations can improve the management of their HR and implement strategies that lead to sustainable competitive advantage. Many well-managed companies have realized that a crucial factor in achieving this advantage is having a strong workforce and efficient management practices (Salamzadeh et al., 2019). The rapid advancement of technology and increased globalization are creating a new economic reality and altering the competitive landscape, making it crucial for companies to establish sustainable competitive advantages (Khatun & Dar, 2021). AI is becoming increasingly important in managing HR in order to develop a sustainable competitive edge. It is being used at three different levels: assisted intelligence, which helps with tasks; augmented intelligence, which enhances the abilities of human workers; and autonomous intelligence, which can perform tasks without human involvement (Charlier & Kloppenburg, 2017).

According to Charlier and Kloppenburg (2017), assisted intelligence involves AI technology to automate repetitive tasks and save time at work, for instance, using chatbots for initial interviews during the hiring procedure. On the other side, augmented intelligence is AI technology that allows for collaboration between humans and machines in making decisions at work. For example, using chatbots equipped with conversational AI can enhance the recruitment experience for candidates by providing personalized, engaging, and real-time interactions across different channels. This involves arranging meetings with potential hires, responding to enquiries from job applicants, and promoting employee recommendations.

Furthermore, autonomous intelligence utilizes AI technology to gather and analyse information independently and make decisions, revolutionizing the work completion processes. For example, it can be applied to select candidates based on specific criteria. The application of AI in HR is very useful as it leads to various positive outcomes, including quick decisions with greater accuracy. This research aimed to examine the different HR functions and identify the AI tools that align with each function to create a comprehensive framework for AI in HR. The framework includes identifying barriers and potential outcomes of implementing AI in HR, as well as identifying relevant AI tools for important HR tasks.

3.2 Artificial Intelligence

AI is a field of computer science that aims to develop machinery/software that can accomplish tasks that call for human cognitive abilities. It also refers to technology that can perform operations requiring a certain level of cognitive ability, meaning a machine that can accomplish what a human can do, to put it differently, a tool trained to do human-like tasks. AI is the capability of a machine or an agent to emulate human intelligence and carry out tasks in various contexts (Negnevitsky, 2005). AI involves developing machines that possess cognitive abilities, and intelligence is the capability of an entity to act appropriately and consistently in its surroundings (Nilsson, 2009). AI is the creation of intelligent systems not of human origin and designed to carry out specific functions (Dwivedi et al., 2021). AI is distinct from traditional software in that it utilizes fast computation, high-quality data, and advanced algorithms to increase the precision and dependability of regular tasks by linking data quality with efficient computing resources. By utilizing a combination of IT tools, web-based applications, analytical models, and many more, businesses can manage their workforce extremely efficiently (Oswal & Narayanappa, 2015). AI can help in making decisions by providing valuable insights. It uses advanced techniques such as ML and algorithms to analyse large amounts of data and reveal patterns that the organization did not previously know (Johnson et al., 2020). AI is currently being applied across various industries and business fields, such as healthcare, finance, manufacturing, human resource management (HRM), education, and more (Morris et al., 2017).

3.3 Evolution of Artificial Intelligence

The AI concept gained attention in the 1950s as people began to explore its potential. However, many science, philosophy, and mathematics experts had previously considered the concept without making it widely known. The idea of AI became prominent only when Alan Turing proposed the Turing test to distinguish between computers and humans. The basis of this experiment was the idea that if humans are capable of storing information and solving problems, machines should also be able to. After 1974, with technological advancements, computers became faster and developed the capability to store more information (Turing, 1950). The field of AI originated in 1956 at Dartmouth College, where the term "artificial intelligence" was first used. Notable figures in the area, including John McCarthy, Marvin Minsky, Oliver Selfridge, Ray Solomonoff, Trenchard More, Claude Shannon, Allen Newell, and Herbert Simon, were present at the event (Brunette et al., 2009). Advances in computing and robotics have resulted in an increased focus on creating intelligent systems with a physical form. However, due to the complex nature of the field, these efforts often need to be connected. Trouble in developing physical robots has led to a shift towards computer representation, known as "artificial general intelligence," in which digital agents in simulated environments try to exhibit intelligent behaviour (Brunette et al., 2009).

The global investment in cognitive and AI technologies is rapidly accelerating, with a compound yearly growth rate (CAGR) of 50.1%. It is a significant increase and reflects these technologies' growing interest and importance. According to a report by NITI Aayog in 2018, this trend is expected to continue. By 2021, the total investment in cognitive and AI technologies will reach $57.6 billion. This highlights these technologies' tremendous potential and value for various industries and sectors. It also points towards the growing need for businesses and organizations to invest in and adopt these technologies to stay competitive in an ever-evolving digital landscape. The use of AI in Indian businesses is limited and slow-moving, with a mere 20% of companies in India presently employing AI in various forms of operation (NITI Aayog, 2018). The study aims to examine the application of AI in HRM tasks. The study aims on identifying the specific AI technologies used in HRM and examining the advantages, barriers, and methods implemented to overcome those barriers.

3.4 Functions of Artificial Intelligence

3.4.1 Machine Learning – Learning from Experience

ML encompasses various methods utilizing data to develop algorithms for predicting outcomes. In business, the most common usage of ML is in "supervised application," where a data scientist trains an algorithm using a specific data set and then evaluates its performance using a chosen metric (Tambe et al., 2019). ML techniques enable the creation of algorithms to evaluate data and make predictions. These predictions can be used to anticipate future outcomes. For example, by examining an employee's behaviour, an algorithm can predict whether or not they are likely to seek new employment opportunities in the near future. It allows companies to take proactive measures to retain valuable employees, such as offering promotions or other incentives.

3.4.2 Deep Learning – Self-Educating Machines

Deep learning is a branch of ML that utilizes neural networks as a critical element in its architecture. These neural networks are structured to imitate the actions of the human brain, allowing them to process and analyse large amounts of complex data effectively. This makes deep learning especially customized for activities including image recognition, natural language processing (NLP), and machine translation, where it can achieve state-of-the-art results. As the amount of data used for training deep learning algorithms increases, the accuracy and efficiency of the resulting model also improve (Meskó et al., 2018). Recent advances in supervised learning in deep networks have resulted in an explosion of applications where large datasets are available (Sejnowski, 2020). Deep learning is utilized in the development of automated systems for both hearing and speech translation, such as home assistance devices that can understand and respond to a user's voice and also can learn and adapt to their preferences.

3.4.3 Cognitive Computing – Making Inferences from the Context

Cognitive computing is a sophisticated technology that combines the power of computer science with the understanding of human cognition or the way the brain processes information. This advanced system is designed to learn and adapt on a large scale, using its knowledge and abilities to reason and make decisions with a specific purpose in mind. Additionally, it can interact with humans naturally, making it simpler for humans to know and work with technology. In short, cognitive computing is the fusion of computer science, and cognitive science attempts to create intelligent methods which could lead to thinking and learning like humans. Cognitive computing systems are designed to mimic the functions of the human mind, allowing them to explain vast amounts of data, discover patterns and correlations, generate hypotheses, generate estimations and inferences, and reach conclusions. These systems rely on self-learning algorithms that use data mining, image and visual recognition, and NLP to solve problems and improve human processes (Dragoni & Rospocher, 2018).

3.4.4 Natural Language Processing – Understanding the Language

NLP is a complex division of AI that aims on creating formulas and models so that computers can know, explain, and develop human language (Hemalatha et al., 2021). NLP includes a broad extent of activities, including text categorization, sentiment explanation, language translation, and speech recognition. The ultimate aim of NLP is to develop computer systems that can interact with humans using natural language, making communication more efficient and seamless. NLP aims to make interacting with machines more natural by training systems to comprehend human language in a specific context and provide appropriate responses. In HRM, NLP could be used with other AI technologies to predict an applicant's potential job performance based on recorded interviews. NLP is also used in digital assistants such as Alexa, Siri, and Cortana to interpret and understand user requests and map them to appropriate actions or tasks (Dickson, 2020). Nevertheless, NLP research has made significant strides in recent years, and the field continues to evolve and improve, with breakthroughs and applications emerging regularly.

3.4.5 Computer Vision – Understanding Images

Computer vision is an area of AI that utilizes ML algorithms to give computers the ability to understand and process visual information, including images, videos, and graphics (Hemlata & Barani, 2019). Recent advancements in computer vision include the ability to identify and classify objects and extract information from different types of data. Additionally, computer vision can detect human emotions, which can be helpful in areas such as HRM by helping managers predict employee turnover (Hemalatha et al., 2021). The advancement of computer vision technology is propelled by a combination of elements, like the availability of high-performing computers, the development of sophisticated algorithm models, and the availability of massive data.

3.5 Application of Artificial Intelligence in Human Resource Management

AI is a cutting-edge technology that can create replicas of human abilities like perception, thinking, and decision-making to enhance human capabilities while overcoming obstacles in the workplace (Jia et al., 2018). AI-empowered human resource tools can enhance employee performance by analysing, predicting, and identifying issues related to staff needs and outcomes, allowing for a more efficient management process (Kumar & Nagrani, 2020). The integration of AI technology is revolutionizing HRM by introducing new capabilities and changing the traditional approach to managing employees within a social group. Human Resource Information System (HRIS) is an essential tool for effectively and efficiently managing a company's HR. It provides the necessary information and data to support informed decision-making by HR professionals, allowing them to manage and optimize the use of their workforce effectively. This can include various tasks such as tracking employee information, managing benefits and compensation, and providing insights into workforce trends and performance. Overall, an HRIS is a vital component of modern HRM, enabling organizations to effectively support their employees and achieve their strategic goals (Masum et al., 2018). The recent implementation of HRIS has created the base for incorporating AI-based software and tools. The human-machine interaction feature developed with AI technology improves management efficiency, streamlining the process of collecting, maintaining, and verifying data necessary for the organization's operations (Merlin & Jayam, 2018). The integration of AI into HR is happening at an accelerated pace. HRM is changing its functions and shifting towards advanced technologies that are fundamentally changing and shaping how organizations manage employees and their relationships with them. As a technological tool, AI automates routine tasks with minimal human involvement. It helps in various stages of the recruitment process, such as screening resumes, sending automated text messages, and checking references. By utilizing the ability of AI to recognize forms, HR can maintain records of the changing requirements and preferences of the employees, giving a competitive edge. AI's ability to estimate future events also enables employees to become better associates with the organization, significantly impacting the organization's objectives (Premnath & Arun 2019).

Compared to other countries, the combination of AI into HR functions in organizations in India is relatively low and could be a lot higher. In India, AI is most commonly used in recruitment, training, and development (Premnath & Arun, 2019). Numerous large-scale companies employ AI technology to take care of talent acquisition operations; nevertheless, some organizations are still in the process of introducing it (Pillai, 2020). In order to eradicate any unconscious prejudice, AI tools must be programmed with the appropriate parameters (Upadhyay & Khandelwal, 2018). AI can effectively handle basic HR tasks, but it is also essential to consider its capabilities in

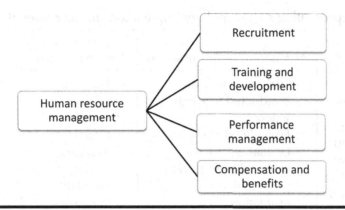

Figure 3.1 Model representing various functions of human resource management. (From Roy, 2021.)

handling complex situations. There are countless motives to employ AI, one of which is that it delivers significant advantages to the organization in a shorter time frame and with more exactness (Pandey & Khaskel, 2019). The combination of automation in HRM tasks such as recruitment, performance evaluation, and talent management will greatly change how they are conducted. With the help of data analytics and digitization, HR managers will have access to more information, allowing them to make more informed decisions about talent management (Fenech, 2022) (Figure 3.1).

3.6 Recruitment and Selection

One of the most challenging tasks for HR professionals is screening a large number of resumes to find the right candidate for the job. With the use of AI, resumes will be automatically scanned and evaluated, allowing for the elimination of those that do not meet the qualifications for the position. AI-based algorithms can effectively screen resumes and identify the most suitable candidates for the job (Garg et al., 2018). A chatbot application can enhance candidates' experience by frequently providing updated information and recommendations. Additionally, AI-powered software can evaluate candidates in audio-video format, assessing factors such as their language usage, speech, nonverbal communication, and other characteristics necessary for the job (Bhardwaj et al., 2020). Chatbots are software that imitates human communication and can be employed to communicate with job applicants in real-time. They can furnish tailored replies to the candidates via text or email and give the recruiters feedback about the applicant's experience

Table 3.1   Representing AI Technology Implications in Recruitment and Selection

HRM Functions	AI Technology Implications	AI Tools and Service Providers	Adoption
Recruitment and selection 1. Screening 2. Testing and assessment 3. Interviewing 4. Background checking 5. Selecting candidates	1. Evaluate interviews conducted through video 2. Evaluate online evaluations such as personality evaluations, programming evaluations, and language evaluations 3. Use automated tools and data analysis to improve the selection process for job candidates 4. Research a candidate's social media presence 5. Utilize interactive games to evaluate a candidate's skills	1. HireVue 2. Koru 3. Watson Candidate Assistant 4. Siri and Alexa 5. SnapHR 6. Pymetrics	1. Companies such as TCS, Wipro, and Flipkart

Source: Pillai (2020).

(Upadhyay & Khandelwal, 2018; Pandey & Bahukhandi, 2022). Companies that utilize AI in the recruitment process majorly focus on three main areas: chatbots/customer relationship management tools, automation of administrative tasks, and software for screening resumes and videos (See Table 3.1). These are among the most popular applications of AI in recruitment (Albert, 2019).

3.7 Training and Development

The need for new skills in the workplace is constantly evolving, and AI technology is being used to develop applications that can recommend video or learning resources related to job tasks and experience. These programmes can analyse instructional documentation and generate small-scale learning programmes. Additionally, AI-based personal learning systems, such as converting written materials into visual formats, are becoming increasingly important. The use of AI in employee engagement and learning is expected to lead to new and innovative ways of training employees (Bhardwaj et al., 2020). AI technologies can help streamline the training process by

Table 3.2   Representing AI Technology Implications in Training and Development

HRM Functions	AI Technology Implications	AI Tools and Service Providers	Adoption
Training and development 1. Career planning 2. Talent mentoring 3. Upskilling/reskilling	1. Personalized course suggestions 2. Adaptive learning path suggestions 3. Track progress on chosen career journeys	1. Eightfold AI 2. Shoox 3. Fuel50	1. Companies such as Infosys, Wipro, and Accenture

Source: Authors' creation.

automatically collecting and analysing data on student progress. This data can be used to quickly assess the effectiveness of the training and provide insights for training managers, saving them time and allowing them to make informed decisions about the training programme (Jia et al., 2018). AI can enhance the delivery of training material by personalizing it with the help of an AI assistant, making it more effective (See Table 3.2). AI systems in training and development can identify essential factors, use existing measurement methods or create new ones to determine the value and impact of training programmes on the business. This feedback can be used to continuously improve the organization's training programmes (Maity, 2019).

3.8 Performance Management

The main objective of performance appraisal is to evaluate the success of a business by linking short-term operational goals with long-term strategies. This approach considers the company's overall vision and day-to-day operations. The performance appraisal method should ensure that the evaluation of procedures and strategies is in sync (Kiradoo et al., 2021). Evaluating individual performance can be challenging for organizations due to bias in the workplace. AI can help reduce and correct these biases by providing feedback. AI-based applications evaluate individual and team goals and assess employee collaboration. Companies are employing AI to optimize their operations and manage their staff by compiling data from various sources, including employee satisfaction, performance indicators, and factors contributing to employee turnover (See Table 3.3). AI can also predict performance indicators for high-performing employees and those who may need to switch roles

Table 3.3   Representing AI Technology Implications in Performance Management

HRM Function	AI Technology Implications	AI Tools and Service Providers	Adoption
1. Performance appraisal	1. Ensuring that team and individual objectives align with the main objectives of the organization 2. Encouraging ongoing communication, providing feedback, and recognizing achievements to support skill development and progress towards goals 3. Monitoring performance in real-time to gain a better understanding of employee capabilities 4. Utilizing data analysis to gain actionable insights into the workforce and the effectiveness of programmes	1. Betterworks 2. Inspire 3. Eloomi	1. Companies such as Infosys, Deloitte, and Oracle

Source: Authors' creation.

(Johnson et al., 2020). Organizations can use AI to scan employee records stored in the HRIS to identify which current employees are qualified for open positions. AI software can evaluate key factors related to employee success to determine which employees should be promoted, thus increasing internal mobility within the organization (Chattopadhyay, 2020).

3.9 Compensation and Benefits

In the current job market, organizations are facing significant challenges in recruiting and retaining highly skilled and talented employees due to increased competition (Tajpour et al., 2021). To successfully attract and

Table 3.4 Representing AI Technology Implications in Compensation Management

HRM Function	AI Technology Implications	AI Tools and Service Providers
Compensation management	1. Salary management 2. Bonus management 3. Long-term incentive and bonus deferral 4. Equal pay and transparency	1. Beqom 2. Carta 3. Curo Compensation Management

Source: Authors' creation.

retain top-notch employees in today's competitive job market, employers need to provide fair and suitable compensation for the positions they offer. This requires leaders to be strategic and aware of industry trends. As HR continues to evolve, it is important to re-evaluate the way compensation is determined. Companies need to consider a broader range of data to create a strategy that fits their workforce and takes into account differences in roles, skills, and expectations. Using tracking and monitoring software can aid in automating the process of determining compensation and benefits based on factors such as hours worked, check-ins, and job tasks (Table 3.4). This allows for more accurate and fair compensation for the employees (Roy, 2021).

3.10 Benefits of Implementing Artificial Intelligence in HRM

Utilizing AI technology to enhance the performance of HRM is a current trend for future progress (Chakraborty et al., 2020). According to Nawaz (2020), there are nine key areas of HRM function where industries can implement AI to improve efficiency and effectiveness in meeting customer needs. Incorporating technology allows the industry to exceed expectations and meet the needs of customers and employees, resulting in improved productivity for the organization.

AI is a novel technology recently introduced to HRM. Despite being new, it has many benefits and has become a valuable tool in HRM. Although AI may not possess humans' emotional and cognitive capabilities, it has demonstrated its usefulness in the realm of HRM by providing the ability to analyse, forecast, and diagnose through AI-based HR applications, making it a valuable asset for any organization (Matsa & Gullamajji, 2019). Paying attention to employee feedback is crucial (Salamzadeh et al., 2019); this can be achieved through chat rooms and message boards that address employee concerns, and multiple applications have been developed to resolve issues for employees and customers quickly. Technology has become integral to HRM (Garg et al., 2018) and is now used to manage various HR functions. As technology advances, AI will become more advanced and efficient. In the future, AI may fully replace HR. Some benefits of AI include the following:

- Reducing workload for administrative staff in an organization
- Assisting in finding the best-suited employee for the job
- Helping to determine employee retention rates in the workplace
- Lowering the risk of errors and streamlining workflow
- Eliminating biases in HR decision-making
- Providing digital assistance
- Automating queries

3.11 Barriers to Adopting Artificial Intelligence in HRM

A major obstacle for organizations looking to implement digital transformation is figuring out how to transition from their current state to a more technologically advanced one. To fully take advantage of digital technology and digital transformation, creating a comprehensive digital plan is advisable to outline the organization's vision, priorities, opportunities, and actions (Ahmad et al., 2021). Many organizations have wasted resources by implementing the wrong technology for their needs. However, with a strong understanding of the various technologies available, companies can more effectively identify which technology will best meet their needs, who to partner with for implementation, and how quickly a system can be implemented (Davenport & Ronanki, 2018). AI can assist HR in addressing one of the most significant challenges they face today, which is developing and implementing strategies for improvement, by providing specific recommendations on how to address these issues promptly (Murgai, 2018). Some obstacles that can impede the integration of AI in HR include the following:

- Financial constraints can limit the implementation of tools to assist HR in administrative tasks.
- A shortage of skilled and trained personnel can be costly and challenging to acquire.

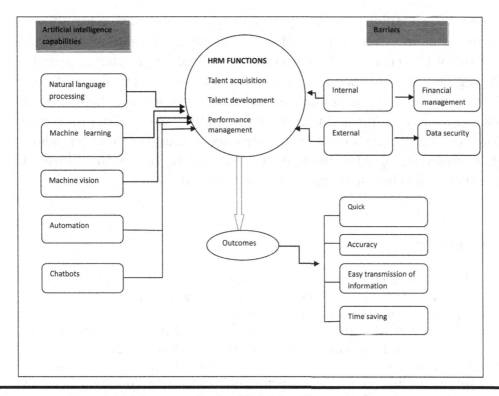

Figure 3.2 Conceptual framework of artificial intelligence in human resource management. (Authors' Creation.)

■ Privacy issues, where confidential HR data must be kept secure and only accessible to authorized individuals.
■ The need for ongoing maintenance as AI, like other advanced technologies, requires ongoing learning and updates to its integration capabilities.
■ Limited data availability due to the increasing trend of HR departments using Software as a Service (SaaS) (Figure 3.2).

3.12 Discussion and Conclusion

Integrating AI-based technologies with HR practices is seen to improve organizational performance significantly. With the increased competition and changes in the business environment, companies need help attracting and retaining top talents and a robust system. As a result, HRM is shifting away from traditional tasks such as hiring and evaluations and moving towards more advanced techniques like automation, augmented intelligence, robotics, and AI. Incorporating AI in HR processes will significantly change how HR functions in various organizations. Currently, AI is rapidly transforming the field of HR, creating job opportunities, simplifying recruitment, and offering new and advanced solutions to various issues. The use of AI in HR systems allows organizations to decrease expenses, simplify processes, boost efficiency, eliminate bias, save time, and reduce employee turnover. However, organizations must ensure data security and employee readiness when implementing AI technology. A policy for the collection and use of data should also be established and implemented.

References

Ahmad, A., Alshurideh, M., Al Kurdi, B., Aburayya, A., & Hamadneh, S. (2021). Digital transformation metrics: a conceptual view. *Journal of Management Information and Decision Sciences*, 24(7), 1–18.

Albert, E. T. (2019). AI in talent acquisition: a review of AI-applications used in recruitment and selection. *Strategic HR Review*, 18(5), 215–221.

Bhardwaj, G., Singh, S. V., & Kumar, V. (2020, January). An empirical study of artificial intelligence and its impact on human resource functions. In *2020 International Conference on Computation, Automation and Knowledge Management (ICCAKM)*, 47–51.

Brunette, E. S., Flemmer, R. C. & Flemmer, C. L. (2009). A review of artificial intelligence. *2009 4th International Conference on Autonomous Robots and Agents*. IEEE, 2009

Chakraborty, S., Giri, A., Aich, A., & Biswas, S. (2020). Evaluating the influence of artificial intelligence on human resource management using PLS-SEM (Partial least squares-structural equation modeling). *International Journal of Scientific and Technology Research*, 9(3), 5876–5880.

Charlier, R., & Kloppenburg, S. (2017). Artificial intelligence in HR: a no-brainer. Retrieved May 3, 2023, from https://www.pwc.nl

Chattopadhyay, P. (2020). A study on various applications of artificial intelligence (AI) in the field of human resource management (HRM*). International Journal of Advanced Research in Science, Communication, and Technology (IJARSCT)*, 11(2), 81–94.

Davenport, T. H., & Ronanki, R. (2018). Artificial intelligence for the real world. *Harvard Business Review*, 96(1), 108–116.

Dickson, B. (2020, December 28). *DeepMind's big losses, and the questions around running an AI lab*. VentureBeat. https://venturebeat.com/ai/deepminds-big-losses-and-the-questions-around-running-an-ai-lab/

Dragoni, M., & Rospocher, M. (2018). Applied cognitive computing: challenges, approaches, and real-world experiences. *Progress in Artificial Intelligence*, 7(4), 249–250.

Dwivedi, Y. K., Hughes, L., Ismagilova, E., Aarts, G., Coombs, C., Crick, T., Duan, Y., Dwivedi, R., Edwards, J., Eirug, A., Galanos, V., Ilavarasan, P. V., Janssen, M., Jones, P., Kar, A. K., Kizgin, H., Kronemann, B., Lal, B., Lucini, B., Medaglia, R., Le Meunier-FitzHugh, K., Le Meunier-FitzHugh, L. C., Misra, S., Mogaji, E., Sharma, S. K., Singh, J. B., Raghavan, V., Raman, R., Rana, N. P., Samothrakis, S., Spencer, J., Tamilmani, K., Tubadji, A., Walton, P., & Williams, M. D. (2021). Artificial Intelligence (AI): multidisciplinary perspectives on emerging challenges, opportunities, and agenda for research, practice and policy. International Journal of Information Management, 57(1), 19–38.

Fenech, R. (2022). Human resource management in a digital era through the lens of next-generation human resource managers. *Journal of Management Information and Decision Sciences*, 25(1), 1–10.

Garg, V., Srivastav, S., & Gupta, A. (2018, October). Application of artificial intelligence for sustaining green human resource management. In *2018 International Conference on Automation and Computational Engineering (ICACE)*, 113–116. IEEE.

Hemalatha, A., Kumari, P. B., Nawaz, N., & Gajenderan, V. (2021, March). Impact of artificial intelligence on recruitment and selection of information technology companies. In *2021 International Conference on Artificial Intelligence and Smart Systems (ICAIS)*, 60–66. IEEE.

Hemlata, A., & Barani, P. (2019). Perception towards artificial intelligence in human resources management practices –with reference to IT companies in Chennai. *International Journal of Recent Technology and Engineering (IJRTE)*, 8(4), 61–65.

Jia, Q., Guo, Y., Li, R., Li, Y., & Chen, Y. (2018, June). A conceptual artificial intelligence application framework in human resource management. In *Proceedings of the International Conference on Electronic Business*, 106–114.

Johnson, R. D., Stone, D. L., & Lukaszewski, K. M. (2020). The benefits of e-HRM and AI for talent acquisition. *Journal of Tourism Futures*, 7(1), 40–52.

Khatun, A., & Dar, S. N. (2021). The challenges and coping strategies of KM implementation in HEIs: an empirical investigation. *International Journal of Asian Business and Information Management*, 12(4), 45–58.

Kiradoo, G., Hashim, N. A. A. N., Ramlee, S. I. F., & Ashifa, K. M. (2021). A comprehensive study of performance appraisal of the business entity. *Journal of Management Information and Decision Sciences*, 24, 1–10.

Kumar, B. S. P., & Nagrani, K. (2020). Artificial intelligence in human resource management. *JournalNX*, ICSSR Issue, 106–118.

Maity, S. (2019). Identifying opportunities for artificial intelligence in the evolution of training and development practices. *The Journal of Management Development*, 38(8), 651–663.

Masum, A. K. M., Beh, L. S., Azad, M. A. K., & Hoque, K. (2018). Intelligent human resource information system (i-HRIS): a holistic decision support framework for HR excellence. *The International Arab Journal of Information Technology*, 15(1), 121–130.

Matsa, P., & Gullamajji, K. (2019). To study impact of artificial intelligence on human resource management. *International Research Journal of Engineering and Technology*, 6(8), 1229–1238.

Merlin, R., & Jayam, R. (2018). Artificial intelligence in human resource management. *International Journal of Pure and Applied Mathematics*, 119(17), 1891–1895.

Meskó, B., Hetényi, G., & Győrffy, Z. (2018). Will artificial intelligence solve the human resource crisis in healthcare? *BMC Health Services Research*, 18(1), 1–4.

Morris, K. C., Schlenoff, C., & Srinivasan, V. (2017). Guest editorial a remarkable resurgence of artificial intelligence and its impact on automation and autonomy. *IEEE Transactions on Automation Science and Engineering*, 14(2), 407–409.

Murgai, A. (2018). Role of artificial intelligence in transforming human resource management. *International Journal of Trend in Scientific Research and Development*, 2(3), 877–881.

Nawaz, N. (2020). Exploring artificial intelligence applications in human resource management. *Journal of Management Information and Decision Sciences*, 23(5), 552–563.

Negnevitsky, M. (2005). *Artificial intelligence: a guide to intelligent systems*. Pearson Education. 364–368.

Nilsson, N. J. (2009). *The quest for artificial intelligence*. Cambridge University Press. 394–398.

Niti Aayog (2018), National Strategy for Artificial Intelligence (https://www.niti.gov. in/sites/default/files/2023-03/National-Strategy-for-Artificial-Intelligence.pdf)

Oswal, N., & Narayanappa, G. (2015). Evolution of HRM to E-HRM to achieve organizational effectiveness and sustainability. *International Journal of Business Administration and Management Research*, 1(2), 22–27.

Pandey, S., & Bahukhandi, M. (2022). Applicants' perception towards the application of AI in recruitment process. In *2022 Proceedings of the International Conference on Interdisciplinary Research in Technology and Management*.

Pandey, S., & Khaskel, P. (2019). Application of AI in human resource management and Gen Y's reaction. *International Journal of Recent Technology and Engineering (IJRTE)*, 8(4), 10325–10331.

Pandey, S., Ruhela, V., & Ruhela, S. (2021). Precursors and ramifications of creativity on innovation in product design teams-a study on Indian information technology sector. *Journal of Physics: Conference Series*, 1860(1), 012014.

Pillai, R. (2020). Adoption of artificial intelligence for talent acquisition in IT organizations. *Benchmarking*, 27(9), 2599–2629.

Premnath, E., & Arun, A. (2019). Artificial intelligence in human resource management: a qualitative study in the Indian context. *Journal of Xi'an University of Architecture & Technology*, XI-X11, 1193–1205.

Radovic, A., & Badawy, S. M. (2020). Technology use for adolescent health and wellness. *Pediatrics*, 145(Supplement_2), S186–S194.

Roy, U. (2021). Evolving uses of Artificial Intelligence for HRM during COVID-19: Bangladesh perspective. *Scopia International Journal for Science, Commerce & Arts (SIJSCA)*, 1(5), 18–25.

Salamzadeh, A., Tajpour, M., & Hosseini, E. (2019). Corporate entrepreneurship in the University of Tehran: does human resource management matter? *International Journal of Knowledge-Based Development*, 10(3), 276–292.

Sejnowski, T. J. (2020). The unreasonable effectiveness of deep learning in artificial intelligence. *Proceedings of the National Academy of Sciences*, 117(48), 30033–30038.

Tajpour, M., Salamzadeh, A., & Hosseini, E. (2021). Job satisfaction in IT department of Mellat Bank: does employer brand matter. *IPSI BgD Transactions on Internet Research*, 17(1), 15–21.

Tambe, P., Cappelli, P., & Yakubovich, V. (2019). Artificial intelligence in human resources management: challenges and a path forward. *California Management Review*, 61(4), 15–42.

Turing, A. M. (1950). Mind – a quarterly review of psychology and philosophy. *Computing Machinery and Intelligence*, 59(236).

Upadhyay, A. K., & Khandelwal, K. (2018). Applying artificial intelligence implications for recruitment. *Strategic HR Review*, 17(5), 255–258.

Chapter 4

Adoption and Impact of Blockchain Technology on Employee Life Cycle

Suruchi Pandey

Symbiosis International University, Pune, India

Sanjay Pandey

Career Launcher, Pune, India

4.1 Introduction

As the global population grows and companies gravel with an ever increasing demand for qualified workers, human resource management (HRM) has become a critical area of focus and as organizations look for innovative ways to improve the way they manage talent, the emergence of blockchain technology offers exciting new possibilities that have the potential to revolutionize the way people work.

There is a wide range of technologies being utilized in businesses. However, there needs to be more information available regarding how and where these technologies are being used to employ, engage, and empower people. One of the primary objectives of this study is to give a descriptive snapshot of the adoption of blockchain technologies over people management function, thereby the impact it will cause. The employee life cycle perspective is being applied to further structure this discussion.

DOI: 10.4324/9781003372622-4

Blockchain technology was originally developed for using the financial industry but has broader applications that can be used in wide range of industries including HRM. Companies can utilize blockchain applications for a number of purposes such as meeting the hiring process, verifying credentials, or improving data security.

Blockchain technology enables the storage of data in blocks, linking it together in a chain and making it accessible to the user on a dynamic basis. Gartner predicted the blockchain technology market would be approximately three trillion. By 2022, 40% of the organizations will be using it. The current study is a curious investigation to know the adoption of blockchain in various aspects of employee life cycles.

Blockchain works on a system that records information in a way that is difficult to copy, edit, and hack for unethical purposes. Hence, it provides systematic, sustainable, safe, and secure data management of massive data sets. The security element uses the owners' digital sign or key to access data saved in digital nodes. The efficiency of time is at god's speed for blockchain transactions at a way too cheaper cost. "Blockchain has the characteristics of decentralisation, immutability, openness, and traceability" (Wang, 2022).

Staying up with the competition and prospering is crucial in the continuously changing global world economy. Nowadays, one of the most crucial determinants of economic advantage is founded on human resource (HR) initiatives by attracting and maintaining competent individuals.

The Internet and other growing technology have assisted in recruiting to retaining suitable individuals for an organization. Tech space is getting better over time. Blockchain is upcoming and promising in the people management space.

Data is the new currency for businesses nowadays and the entire competition strategy is moving digital. Blockchain technology offers reliable solutions to data management systems. The usage of blockchain has gained momentum over the past few years, and it is emerging as predicted to dominate the future way of doing business. Its usage is well-established in marketing, supply chain technology for purchasing and sales, data security, finance, and manufacturing functions (Coita, Abrudan & Matei, 2019). Three fundamental functions that make blockchain functioning are as follows:

1. Secure keys with cryptographic
2. Shared ledger with peer to peer
3. Means for storage and transaction

Blockchain offers fundamental technology, and its adoption at more significant levels across the globe will revolutionize the mode of businesses operations as well as tapping the potential usage in people management areas. This article explores the options for blockchain usage in employee management functions. The objective of the chapter is:

1. To list the possible application of blockchain technology across the employee life cycle
2. To review the blockchain application in improving employee experience throughout the employee life cycle

The article will be helpful to non-managerial and non-HR professionals (beginners and practitioners) in understanding blockchain technology adoption scope and usage. It may encourage early adopters to make a successful case of implementing blockchain technology in their processes. Researchers adopted secondary data study with the aim of current articles, research papers, and white papers to evaluate the adoption of blockchain technology in managing people function. The employee life cycle is the central theme for this discussion to discuss the adoption and impact of blockchain technology. Most of the articles screened talk about the futuristic view of its adoption into business; however, there are rarely any success cases discussed in the literature. Big companies such as IBM Garage and AWS Blockchain have developed solutions for other corporates (Eliack 2022). The number of start-ups adopting HR-based solutions is encouraging among the start-ups offering blockchain technology HR solutions for employee management, Beowulf, BeSure, Etch, eXo platform, Gospel Technology, Job.com, Lympo, Peoplewave, Vault platform, and WurkNow (BasuMallick, 2021).

4.2 Employee Life Cycle

The employee life cycle model identifies and expresses the various and most crucial stages employees go through as they engage with their company. There are six distinct stages in employee's life cycle: attraction, recruitment, onboarding, development, retention, and separation (Nosratabadi, Zahed, Ponkratov & Kostyrin, 2022). Figure 4.1 is pictorial presentation of employee life cycle.

Figure 4.1 Pictorial presentation of employee life cycle stages.

The employee life cycle begins with attraction, moving towards recruitment, onboarding, learning and development, performance improvement, reward and recognition, and exit.

Sulaiman, Alamsyah, and Wulansari's (2022) paper seeks to "enhance the relationship among recruitment entities by adopting a transparent and incorruptible decentralized autonomous organisation (DAO) model powered by blockchain technology" (Figure 4.2).

Arora (2021), in the LinkedIn article, mentioned that the usage of blockchain technology can mitigate bad hiring costs. It can be used in employment history, credential verification, and routine tasks such as payroll tracking and training. However, data security and entry of erroneous data is an irreversible concern.

The PWC report 2021 mentioned, "The prize is so great that blockchain will inevitably happen – and will ultimately become invisible because it is so frictionless". Data usage and protection policies will be another advantage of using blockchain technology, sourcing, productivity gains, and cross-border payments.

The Accenture (2017) report elaborates that infrastructure costs can be reduced by 30% by utilizing blockchain technologies in various functions.

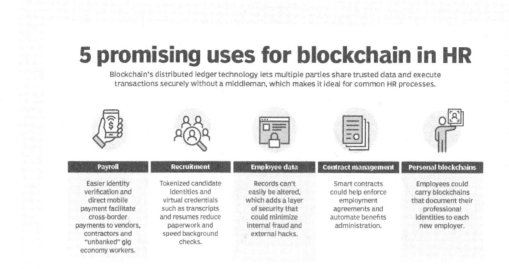

Figure 4.2 Blockchain across the employee life cycle. (From Baker, 2021, 5 Promising uses of blockchain in HR: techtarget online.)

PWC (2018) Global survey of 600 executives on blockchain disclosed 84% of respondents have already established connections with blockchain in their operations and businesses. Marketsandmarkets (2023) report on blockchain market informed compound annual growth rate of blockchain market to be around 66 % in coming five years. The market will expand to 94.7 billion US dollar by 2027 comparing to 7.4 billion US dollar in 2022.

"A reported 75% of HR managers have identified a lie on a CV. With nearly 20% of hiring managers also reporting they spend less than 30 seconds looking at a CV, it is impossible to know how many fabrications go undetected"

(Careerbuilder 2017)

They enhance employee experience from onboarding to performance feedback, benefit claims, insurance claims, reporting system, timesheets, and productivity calculations. Currently, claims take 90 days; this can be reduced. Organizations have outsourced this function to a great extent; however, with blockchain technology, this could be streamlined, and employees' payment of automated taxes and avoid unnecessary audits, contributions to PF and ESI could also be made timely. It can be utilized so that companies can create their own currency and save huge transaction charges for cross-border transactions.

"The blockchain platforms can help with solving tasks of HR service in the search and selection of candidates" (Levitskaya, Pokrovskaia, & Rodionova, 2022). In an automated recruiting system, a recruiter would post a job opening on an online job board and posting would be automatically submitted to the relevant candidates based on their profile information. Candidates would then submit their resume rather filling the application form. Once the resume is submitted, a smart contract would be created based on the information provided by the candidate including all the details such as the salary started and other details negotiated between the candidate and the employer. The contract would then be stored in the blocks and database where it can be viewed and accessed by either party at any time in the future. The fully automatic hiring process illuminates the need for human involvement and dramatically reduces the cost involved in running and HR department. In addition to cost saving, the automated recruitment system also increases efficiency and eliminates the possibility of fraud as all the details relating to the contract are securely stored in the centralized network that no single party controls.

Future of HR is smart HR that uses blockchain technology extensively in all HR and operations functions (Srivastava et al., 2022). Use of smart contracts can automatically process while reducing cost and eliminating potential fraud. Smart contracts are programs that are self-executing without the need of third party to verify the terms of a contract between the parties involved. They are also referred to "smart agreements". They eliminate the need for manual intervention and enable both parties to transact in a secure transparent manner.

Tracking and managing the performance of employees will be easier for managers with greater transparency (Nurhasanah, Prameswari, & Fachrunnisa, 2021), leading to better career paths.

Mishra and Venkatesan (2021) concluded that HR and non-HR professionals know blockchain technology usage in resource management. Both segments of employees think alike of its utility in the organization.

Kisi (2022) detailed candidates' complete work history, performance, layoff, rewards, transfer promotion, and career movements are mapped. Easy verification of candidates from a previous employer, career progressions, and academic credentials is possible. Blockchain can make 360-degree feedback from various stakeholders. Appraisal inputs of various stages and periodicity can be easily tracked for meaningful full discussions and enabling decisions.

Implementing blockchain technology in HR offers prominent attributes such as decentralization, anonymity, immutability, transparency, reliability, and security that can go a long way in various processes required for legal compliance and the safety of employees. It could be sexual harassment (Rahman, Azam, & Chowdhury, 2022), grievance procedures, or customer complaints.

Blockchain offers extensive usage in aligning training needs and provides completion certificates for the forthcoming appraisal process. HR departments are the prime movers in blockchain adoption (Mohammad Saif and Islam 2022). This automates the training process. The evaluation of HR process and measurements to the HR matrix is carried out through blockchain technology. Various ratios, percentages, and dashboard access to stakeholders will be handy. Companies can use the blockchain-based credential verification service to quickly and easily verify academic qualifications and professional certifications without worrying about the risk of identity theft and fraud. The main advantage of using blocks and technology for credential verification is that it provides a decentralize means of verifying the academic qualifications of applicants since no central authority or government agency is responsible for such verification (Rhemananda, Simbolon, & Fachrunnisa 2021).

4.2.1 Challenges

It is posited that blockchain technology's adoption speed in HRM and employee life cycle needs to be much faster to exploit its full potential. However, specific challenges in its way are acting as roadblocks. Following are a few pointers author presents as the challenge of minor nature, but they deserve careful consideration from the adopters.

Understanding compliance risks from various countries is critical. Since the advantage of blockchain is in international transactions and deployment of resources, legal team will have to study and understand what lies ahead in such technology implementation.

Counter-party/third-party involvement and data sharing are other issues that deserve careful address.

Data privacy approvals and legal framework due to distributed ledger are also the legal arena of concern. The human element cannot be ignored, i.e. employees' comfort in sharing personal data, which could involve data of financial, social, and personal nature. (Michailidis, 2018, Salah, Ahmed & ElDahshan, 2020)

Few researchers have indicated scalability as a concern with blockchain transactions. Scalability to be able to perform 7 and 15 transactions per second. However, enterprise blockchains such as Hyperledger Fabric claim 3,500 transactions per second (Perboli et al., 2018; Conti, et al., 2019; Chillakuri & Attilli, 2022).

Ramachandran, Babu, and Murugesan (2022), in their study, mentioned that training and development in this discipline continue to account for a significant percentage of contribution in enabling the success of blockchain technology implementation.

Acceptance from employees in this is a massive concern, as raised by this study. This transition will have to be smooth. In the era of multi-culture, multiple generational, diversified, gig employees, HR departments will have to involve people in this transition.

4.3 Conclusion

This decade has seen the adoption and absorption of technology at Godspeed. Post-COVID technology adoptions have become smoother. Solutions such as blockchain are needed to solve present employee management-related concerns. However, new legal and regulatory developments are expected in this direction to protect employees' data.

References

Accenture (2017). Accenture News Room article online retrieved from https://newsroom.accenture.com/news/blockchain-technology-could-reduce-investment-banks-infrastructure-costs-by-30-percent-according-to-accenture-report.htm

Arora, R. (2021). Blockchain Technology in Human Resource Management, Published on October 10, 2021. https://www.linkedin.com/pulse/blockchain-technology-human-resources-raghav-arora/

Baker, P. (2021). Blockchain HR technology: 5 use cases impacting human resources. https://www.techtarget.com/searchhrsoftware/tip/Blockchain-HR-technology-5-use-cases-impacting-human-resources

BasuMallick, C. (2021). 10 Start-ups Using Blockchain to Answer Key HR Questions in 2020. https://www.spiceworks.com/hr/hr-strategy/articles/top-blockchain-hr-startups/

Careerbuilder (2017), New career builder Press release. https://press.careerbuilder.com/2017-09-14-75-of-HR-Managers-Have-Caught-a-Lie-on-a-Resume-According-to-a-New-CareerBuilder-Survey

Chillakuri, B. and Attili, V.S.P. (2022). Role of blockchain in HR's response to new-normal. International Journal of Organizational Analysis, 30(6), 1359–1378. https://doi.org/10.1108/IJOA-08-2020-2363

Coita, D.C., Abrudan, M.M. and Matei, M.C. (2019). Effects of the Blockchain Technology on Human Resources and Marketing: An Exploratory Study. In: Kavoura, A., Kefallonitis, E., and Giovanis, A. (eds) Strategic Innovative Marketing and Tourism. Springer Proceedings in Business and Economics. Springer, Cham. https://doi.org/10.1007/978-3-030-12453-3_79

Conti, M., Gangwal, A. and Todero, M. (2019), Blockchain trilemma solver algorand has dilemma over undecidable messages, Proceedings of 14th International Conference of Availability Reliability and Security, 16, 1–8.

Eliack, E. (2022). Is HR ready for blockchain? https://dataconomy.com/2022/06/blockchain-in-hr/#:~:text=IBM%20Garage%20created%20a%20private,employers%20or%20across%20the%20network

Kisi, N. (2022). Exploratory research on the use of blockchain technology in recruitment. Sustainability, 14, 10098. https://doi.org/10.3390/su141610098

Levitskaya, A.N., Pokrovskaia, N.N. and Rodionova, E.A. (2022). Blockchain Platforms as a Tool for Resolving Contradictions in the Labor Market and Improving the Interaction of the Applicant and Employer. Conference of Russian Young Researchers in Electrical and Electronic Engineering (ElConRus), 1698–1703. https://doi.org/10.1109/ElConRus54750.2022.9755491

Marketsandmarkets (2023). Blockchain Market Global Forecast 2023 http://www.marketsandmarkets.com/Market-Reports/blockchain-technology-market-90100890.html

Michailidis, M. (2018). The challenges of AI and blockchain on HR recruiting practices. The Cyprus Review, 30(2).

Mishra, H. and Venkatesan, M. (2021). Blockchain in human resource management of organisations: An empirical assessment to gauge HR and non-HR perspective. Journal of Organizational Change Management, 34(2), 525–542. https://doi.org/10.1108/JOCM-08-2020-0261

Mohammad Saif, A.N. and Islam, M.A. (2022). Blockchain in human resource management: A systematic review and bibliometric analysis. Technology Analysis & Strategic Management. https://doi.org/10.1080/09537325.2022.2049226

Nosratabadi, S., Zahed, R.K., Ponkratov, V.V. and Kostyrin, E.V. (2022). Artificial intelligence models and employee lifecycle management: A systematic literature review, Organizacija, 55(3), 181–198. https://doi.org/10.2478/orga-2022-0012 https://www.gartner.com/en/articles/what-is-blockchain https://www.simplilearn.com/tutorials/blockchain-tutorial/blockchain-technology https://hbr.org/2017/01/the-truth-about-blockchain

Nurhasanah, Y., Prameswari, D. and Fachrunnisa, O. (2021). Blockchain-Based Solution for Effective Employee Management. In: Pattnaik, P.K., Sain, M., Al-Absi, A.A. and Kumar, P. (eds) Proceedings of International Conference on Smart Computing and Cyber Security. SMARTCYBER 2020. Lecture Notes in Networks and Systems, vol 149. Springer, Singapore. https://doi.org/10.1007/978-981-15-7990-5_14

Perboli, G., Musso, S. and Rosano, M. (2018). Blockchain in logistics and supply chain: a lean approach for designing real-world use cases, IEEE Access, 6, 62018–62028

PWC (2018). PWC Global Blockchain Survey 2018: Blockchain is here. What's your move? https://www.pwc.ch/en/insights/hr/how-blockchain-can-impact-hr-and-the-world-of-work.html

PWC (2021). How blockchain technology could impact HR and the world of work. https://www.pwc.ch/en/insights/hr/how-blockchain-can-impact-hr-and-the-world-of-work.html

Rahman, M.M., Azam, M. and Chowdhury, F. (2022). Secure complaint management system against women harassment at workplace using blockchain technology. International Journal of Electrical and Computer Engineering Systems, 13, 209–217. https://doi.org/10.32985/ijeces.13.3.6

Ramachandran, R., Babu, V. and Murugesan, V.P. (2022). The role of blockchain technology in the process of decision-making in human resource management: A review and future research agenda, Business Process Management Journal. https://doi.org/10.1108/BPMJ-07-2022-0351

Rhemananda, H., Simbolon, D.R. and Fachrunnisa, O. (2021). Blockchain Technology to Support Employee Recruitment and Selection in Industrial Revolution 4.0. In: Pattnaik, P.K., Sain, M., Al-Absi, A.A. and Kumar, P. (eds) Proceedings of International Conference on Smart Computing and Cyber Security. SMARTCYBER 2020. Lecture Notes in Networks and Systems, vol 149. Springer, Singapore. https://doi.org/10.1007/978-981-15-7990-5_30

Salah, D., Ahmed, M.H. and ElDahshan, K. (2020). Blockchain Applications in Human Resources Management: Opportunities and Challenges. In: Proceedings of the Evaluation and Assessment in Software Engineering (EASE '20). Association for Computing Machinery, New York, NY, USA, 383–389. https://doi.org/10.1145/3383219.3383274

Srivastava, Y., Ganguli, S., Suman Rajest, S. and Regin, R. (2022). Smart HR Competencies and Their Applications in Industry 4.0. In: Kumar, P., Obaid, A.J., Cengiz, K., Khanna, A. and Balas, V.E. (eds) A Fusion of Artificial Intelligence and Internet of Things for Emerging Cyber Systems. Intelligent Systems Reference Library, vol 210. Springer, Cham. https://doi.org/10.1007/978-3-030-76653-5_16

Sulaiman, R., Alamsyah, A. and Wulansari, P. (2022). Reshaping the Future of Recruitment through Talent Reputation and Verifiable Credentials using Blockchain Technology. 10th International Conference on Information and Communication Technology (ICoICT). 316–321, https://doi.org/10.1109/ICoICT55009.2022.9914891

Wang, T. (2022). A study on the innovative use of blockchain in the human resources service industry. Wireless Communications and Mobile Computing, 2022, 1–11. https://doi.org/10.1155/2022/7798595

Chapter 5

Spurring Organisation Performance through Artificial Intelligence and Employee Engagement: An Empirical Study

G. P. Mishra and K. L. Mishra
Birla Institute of Technology Mesra, Ranchi, Jaipur Campus, India

S. S. Pasumarti

Dr Vishwanath Karad MIT-World Peace University, Pune, India

D. Mukherjee
Jamia Millia Islamia (A Central University), New Delhi, India

A. Pande
Jamnalal Bajaj Institute of Management Studies, Mumbai, India

A. Panda
KLE Technological University, Hubballi, India

DOI: 10.4324/9781003372622-5

5.1 Introduction

We have witnessed an increasing use of artificial intelligence (AI) technology among corporations for managing employees. It is a technology according to which a PC or a system can respond, reason, and have the capacity to detect and identify the atmosphere and surroundings. Computer systems with advanced AI can get involved in recognising, identifying, and retorting in the most complex, energetic, and vibrant environments. According to O'Connor (2016), algorithm management is deployed through AI to manage the employees in the organisation. According to Gerlsbeck (2018) and Kolbjornsrud, Amico, and Thomas (2016), organisations are adopting these systems at a rapid pace to help manage their workforce. Nowadays, organisations are using AI in their human resource (HR) departments as humans are becoming assets at changing rates; therefore, it is evident that innovation will have a lasting impact in the field of HR. The applicant's perception study also reported the positive effect of AI on HR processes on applicants (Pandey & Bahukhandi, 2022).

For this reason, HR experts must prepare themselves for these changes by understanding what innovation is and how it is connected across different capacities. Whereas, in the past, counterfeit insights may have been thought to be an item of science fiction, most experts nowadays get that the appropriation of keen innovation is effectively changing working environments (Pandey, Ruhela, & Ruhela, 2021). There are applications of AI throughout each calling asset's career. Later, established human assets experts accept that AI can show openings for acing modern abilities and picking up and growing their current parts to be more vital inside their organisation. Eighty-one per cent of HR leaders who have taken an interest in the study said that they find it challenging to keep up with the time. As such, it is more vital now than ever for human assets experts to understand how AI is reshaping the industry. Our findings explore what counterfeit insights get involved in, how it is connected to the world of human assets administration, and how HR experts can get ready for the long haul in the field nowadays. Associations are rapidly embracing these answers to help deal with their staff (Gerlsbeck, 2018; Kolbjrnsrud, Amico, & Thomas, 2016; Pandey & Khaskel, 2019). Their allure comes from two unique elements.

To start with, firms presently approach huge amounts of information (enormous information) regarding their business exercises, which might be utilised to illuminate the board's decisions more powerfully and effectively. Second, ventures can now assemble and handle this information progressively because of improvements in AI. Indeed, even in the most convoluted and dynamic business sectors, associations can now integrate the latest data into their navigation. Regardless, computer-based intelligence presents new challenges for employees, who are currently driven and mindful by simulated intelligence.

Employee engagement is critical for an association's well-being and creation, yet it is a significant obstacle that organisations worldwide should overcome. Gallup (2017), the board diary's latest focus on employee engagement, found that 29% of labourers are effectively involved, 54% are not locked in, and 17% are separated. Zeroing in on prescribed procedures and devices that permit employees to bring a full scope of mental, close-to-home, and actual energies to their work jobs is critical considering these issues, which are exacerbated by the presentation and coordination of new advancements like computer-based intelligence into the working environment (Shuck, Adelson, & Reio, 2017).

5.2 Problem Statement

Employee commitment is essential and crucial to the well-being and production of any firm or establishment; however, there is an inordinate amount of research and investigation being conducted by firms across the globe. According to a Gallup (2017) survey report, it was found that 29% of employees are actively engaged, 54% are not engaged, and 17% are disengaged. Therefore, the employees must be trained in the best practices that may include a full range of intellectual, rational, demonstrative, expressive, and physical energies in their effort parts, which is of acute significance (Shuck, Adelson, & Reio, 2017).

Employee attitude is one of the most significant problems for any organisation. The organisation may be in the business of online sales through its website and advertisements. They receive multiple feedback and reviews of their products from all the channels (website and TV channels). Organisations have a limited collection or database of reviews of their products, so it is a challenge for HR to find the attitudes of their employees. It can be done by developing a dashboard through which they can analyse the reviews of their products and do a sentiment analysis of them.

5.3 Research Objectives

The research is based on discovering the role of AI in employee engagement and sentiments that will improve performance levels. The objective of employee sentiments using AI-based text analysis techniques is that the computer reads the employee's sentiments. It can predict reviews as positive or negative based on customer reviews that are predicted with the help of machines. Manually, it is impossible to read every review because they know there are millions of reviews, so they use some software to predict the reviews. It improves sales because, based on customer product reviews, they know what customers want, further facilitating in identifying product faults and improving product quality according to market demand. The software that was required for our study is Python, Pandas, NumPy, Matplotlib, scikit-learn, NLP, Pickle module, WebDriver (chrome driver), Beautiful Soup (BS4), Selenium, and Dash Library.

5.4 Literature Review

5.4.1 Controls for Artificial Intelligence Employees

One should comprehend the crucial aspect of AI and its control over employees. There are two main approaches to employee engagement: Theory X and theory Y of management, according to which one aims to increase employee arrangement by supervising and rewarding, whereas theory Y aims to increase employee engagement by increasing worker satisfaction by giving them more freedom and autonomy in their jobs and reducing their need for supervision (Carson, 2005; Kopelman, Prottas, & Davis, 2008). Each strategy for increasing employee engagement involves using AI management systems to direct, monitor, and reward or punish employee behaviour for increasing employee engagement. This strategy supports the gig economy, such as Uber (Maaravi, et al., 2021). However, it applies to traditional corporations with AI management systems.

Employee behaviour that advances the goals and objectives of the organisation is encouraged through organisational controls (Cardinal, Kreutzer, & Miller, 2017). To manage their workforce, several platform companies use AI management solutions. As an illustration, an AI-powered Uber app that directs the driver by telling them about the organisation and its control using AI management systems is likely crucial.

5.4.1.1 Control of Artificial Intelligence Behaviour

The behaviour of AI management is supervising an employee's job actions to ensure their adherence to specific standards. In general, behaviour controls work best when the company and the personnel clearly understand how a task will be carried out. To ensure staff members abide by corporate regulations, a retail store manager, for instance, can observe how staff members greet and engage with customers. High intrinsic motivation and favourable attitudinal outcomes have been linked to behaviour control. Cardinal technologies frequently control AI activity.

5.4.1.2 Control of Artificial Intelligence Outcomes

By taking the AI outcome, the device is implemented. While outcome control entails assessing workers' performance after the service is provided, behaviour control necessitates direct observation of employees' activities. Monthly or quarterly sales targets and presentation reviews show certain instances of consequences and panels. An example of AI outcome control implemented through a digital platform is Uber's rating system. Uber may suspend certain employees who consistently earn performance ratings below 4.0/5.

5.4.1.3 Trust in Artificial Intelligence

The willingness of a worker to be vulnerable to the organisation's activities can be defined as trust in the organisation (Dirks & Ferrin, 2001; McAllister, 1995). Using this concept as a foundation, imagine a worker exposed to decisions made by the artificial management system. Staff should believe in their AI management system and expect good things to emerge. Trust will be a critical factor in efficiency because of vulnerability and positivity. Social exchange theory frequently explains the benefits of faith and belief (Dirks & Ferrin, 2001).

5.4.1.4 Artificial Intelligence as a Tool for Decision-Making

AI-based technology has exponentially increased the speed and accuracy with which leaders can make choices. It is felt increasingly if the processed data or information is extensive, intricate, or dynamic. Because the human brain will not be able to handle it in this situation, the necessity for intelligent machine help is growing. Technology transforms into a tool that supports human decision-making by limiting human judgement as much as the role of change.

5.4.2 *Employee Engagement*

Employee engagement refers to three factors that show how motivated and committed people are to the company: 1) "Say": Employees speak about the role of change in the environment regarding their employers, co-workers, and jobs. 2) "Stay": Instead of using their current role of change as a temporary transition, employees sincerely aspire to become part of the organisation and wish to remain there for a very long time. 3) "Strive": Workers are prepared to put in extra effort to contribute to the company's success (Hewitt, 2001). Employee engagement is divided into sensual engagement and rational engagement by the Towers organisation, which describes it as "the extent to which workers are willing and capable of assisting businesses in succeeding". The interaction between people and businesses, and the extent to which employees are aware of their individual and departmental responsibilities, is often the focus of rational engagement. Working can result in personal growth and rewards when the staff feels logically engaged. Sensible engagement depends on employee pleasure and the feeling of accomplishment from working for the firm (Fay & Kline, 2011). According to Xiao and Benbasat (2007), employee engagement is defined as a person's commitment to their job, which includes hard work, dedication to the business, loyalty to the boss, and self-assurance.

Employee involvement has been given similar definitions. Rothbard and Patil (2011) defined it as a psychological state of absorption and attentiveness. Kahn (1990) defined it as when employees give themselves to their work physically, mentally, and emotionally. These concepts have been described more recently by HRD researchers as a "role of change leadership". All definitions, when taken overall, include an inspiration and a reaction to that inspiration of some kind. Employees will not exclusively dedicate time and work to their work but they will additionally do it to some extent since they appreciate it. Accordingly, the meaning of employee engagement in this section incorporates both inspiration and enthusiasm.

5.4.2.1 Motivation

The "internal factors that direct, energise, and sustain work-related effort" are known as motivation. According to Chen et al. (2009), motivation is to make and maintain an effort. Humans are driven to work hard to accomplish a goal or purpose of change leadership. Motivational theories demonstrate the way that the significance of objectives and targets can propel individuals to apply exertion during an errand (Kanfer & Ackerman, 1989).

The readiness of an employee to invest energy into finishing their work can be considered a mark of employee inspiration. As per Chen and Kanfer (2006), employee inspiration is critical in a person's and a group's presentation. An employee's level of inspiration and going with exertion fundamentally affects execution, which is the consequence of stress, especially in examinations, taking a gander at social sluggishness or keeping exertion (Alnuaimi, Robert, & Maruping, 2010). As per them, inspiration correlates well with work fulfilment and workgroup maintenance. By and large, critical employee results are emphatically impacted by inspiration.

Goal selection, goal pursuit, and confidence in one's ability to achieve goals are the three main elements of motivation (Chen & Gogus, 2008). Deciding which goal or collection of goals to pursue is known as goal choosing (Parker et al., 2010). Goal striving measures how much effort a worker puts into obtaining a specific target or collecting objectives. Self-efficacy, or the conviction that one can accomplish a goal, affects the energy and perseverance people devote to reaching their goal (Parker et al., 2010). In conclusion, the motivational process that explains a person's effort to obtain a goal comprises self-efficacy, goal selection, and goal striving. Every one of these cycles can be helped by computer-based intelligence.

5.4.3 *Employee Engagement and Employee Performance*

Employee engagement is the state of being actively involved in one's work and is characterised by zeal, commitment, and immersion (Hughes, Robert, Frady, & Arroyos, 2019). Life is the term for having great energy and determination while working. Substantial interest in one's calling and a feeling of importance and excitement are qualities of devotion. A state of complete fixation and satisfied contribution to one's occupation is known as retention. In this manner, persuaded staff usually do the job of progressing authority's high degrees from within. Also, they lose themselves, which makes time pass quickly. Task performance includes, among other things, accomplishing business objectives and giving convincing deal introductions.

Notwithstanding, the viability of their work is still up in the air due to both their creation and the amount and nature of their work (Luthans & Doh, 2012). Currently, three essential classes of lead are composed of a work performance:

Task execution: The manner in which somebody satisfies commitments and takes care of giving labour and products or dealing with authoritative exercises. Most of the obligations referenced are part of the set of working responsibilities.

Participation: The commitment of deeds to the workplace climate includes helping others accomplish hierarchical objectives, treating colleagues well, presenting supportive ideas, and talking well about the work environment.

Counter-efficiency: It incorporates ways of behaving like taking, harming corporate property, acting fiercely towards associates, and neglecting to appear for work. Most overseers accept that gaining ground in the underlying two angles while avoiding the third is essential for good performance. Undoubtedly, even the warmest and most enthusiastic workers cannot do critical work immediately and will not be extraordinary employees. A person who performs focus work fittingly, which is appalling and powerful towards partners, will not be regarded as an extraordinary employee in many firms.

A "connected employee" is fascinated by and excited about their work. Thus, they make a helpful move to propel the standing and interests of the organisation and have a decent mentality towards the organisation and its goals (Hu & Liden, 2014). Gallup (2017) differentiates the three categories of employee engagement levels based on their attitude and behaviour. Actively disengaged employees are those who publicly express their dissatisfaction with the organisation and other employees. They act as company poisoners or like thorns in the flesh. They waste good energy by draining it.

Disengaged workers are those who think like salaried employees. They do not cause harm but also do not offer a more incredible alternative. Ordinary employees have ordinary energy. Employees who are passionate, energetic, and make a meaningful difference are considered to be engaged. Their presence and actions generate more good energy. They determine a company's level of excellence. They commit themselves to the business. They hold the key to a better future. There is an emotional bond between the employee and their work. When performing their jobs, employees may feel content or under stress. It will ultimately moderate the output.

5.5 Hypothesis of the Study

The study's hypotheses, which are put forth to evaluate the assertions made as a part of the theoretical model, are as follows:

H1: AI and employee performance are significantly related.
H2: AI and employee engagement are significantly related.

H3: Employee performance is positively associated with AI.
H4: AI has a positive impact on job engagement.

5.6 Research Methodology

The study is based on exploratory research. This section covers one of the methods utilised to guide the current examination. It is responsible for the test design, instrument development philosophy, test schedule, data gathering methods, and data analysis approaches. The study design: A survey has been used to collect data. Employees of various organisations were supposed to make up the population. Two hundred employees from various organisations were studied for this study. The randomisation of test results is taken into consideration by the random sampling technique, which means that each example has a similar possibility of being chosen to represent the entire population. In research areas, it is regarded as one of the most unique and direct data grouping techniques (probability and experience, mathematics). It considers logical data fusion, which enables investigations to arrive at truthful conclusions. The survey questionnaire was used as a tool to gather the data. A self-created instrument on a Likert scale was used in combination with a structured survey to conduct this experiment. It was a qualitative study design, which was sufficient given the time constraints. Due to the constraint, the sample size was constrained, making it impossible to generalise the findings. The data was gathered using a questionnaire survey instrument.

The domains of AI enablement strategy, core capabilities of AI enablement, employee performance, and work engagement aid in understanding AI enablement practises and their influence on organisational performance. These variables are arranged according to the number of distinct assertions. Using this data for our model training and testing, we uncompressed it and then unzipped it, and its actual or average size was 14.14 GB. This refers to extensive data, and that was, after un-compression or unzip of this data extension of files, which has the extension ".json", JSON format is one of the most popular formats nowadays, like whenever mobile applications, IOT applications, web applications, or machine learning applications are developed. The JSON format is very similar to a Python dictionary (the dictionary format is a key-value pair). The key-value pair format is the same for JSON data. Overall rating: Given by the customer (ratings are scaled from 1 to 5).

5.7 Result and Discussion

The results regarding the effects of AI capabilities on organisation performance through AI and employee engagement validate and establish to the middle- and top-level leaders who use AI that provides diverse outcomes contingent on the type of enhancement and augmentation organisations are looking for. As we know, AI usages are very varied in their characteristics and nature. Therefore, it could be more manageable to comprehend the exact worth and prominence of various operating happenings. The outcome was both an experiment and an excellent occasion for the middle and higher-level leaders as they can categorise strengths and weaknesses that need to be impoverished in their central and crucial parameters to the firms and position them as suitable towards better solutions using AI to improve them. Please see Figure 5.1

From Graph No-1, we find that our score for the linear regression model is 90%. From the above, we see that our study features an extraction and normalisation technique that was applied, and then, using logistic regression, we tested the accuracy of the text data. After testing the model, we created the user interface for this project. For the user interface part's creation, we used a Dash library where the user or client can easily see whether the review is positive or negative. There are two sections in the user interface: The first is the perfectly linearly separable graph. The almost linearly separable section shows the level of positive reviews and percentage or negative reviews and percentage. The second section has a review textbox where the user can type and check any review, showing whether the review about the employee is positive or negative. Please see the computer-generated AI programming Sheet in Figure 5.2 for the same.

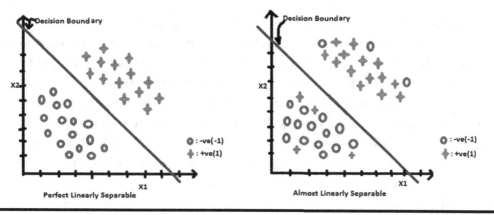

Figure 5.1   Perfect Linearly Separable and Almost Linearly Separable Graph.

```
In [14]: from sklearn.model_selection import train_test_split
    ...: features_train,features_test,labels_train,labels_test =
train_test_split(df['reviewText'],df['Positivity'],random_state=
42)

    ...: from sklearn.feature_extraction.text import
TfidfVectorizer

    ...: vect = TfidfVectorizer(min_df = 5).fit(features_train)

In [15]: features_train_vectorized =
vect.transform(features_train)

    ...: from sklearn.linear_model import LogisticRegression

    ...: model = LogisticRegression ()

    ...: model.fit(features_train_vectorized,labels_train)

    ...: predictions=
model.predict(vect.transform(features_test))
C:\Users\ssingh\anaconda3\lib\site-packages\sklearn\linear_model
\_logistic.py:762: ConvergenceWarning: lbfgs failed to converge
(status=1):
STOP: TOTAL NO. of ITERATIONS REACHED LIMIT.

Increase the number of iterations (max_iter) or scale the data
as shown in:

In [16]: from sklearn.metrics import confusion_matrix

    ...: confusion_matrix(labels_test,predictions)
Out[16]:
array([[60182,  5798],
       [ 7025, 58822]], dtype=int64)

In [17]: from sklearn.metrics import roc_auc_score

    ...: roc_auc_score(labels_test,predictions)
Out[17]: 0.9027190865955793
```

Figure 5.2   Computer-generated AI programming Sheet.

From this AI algorithm, our study features an extraction and normalisation technique that was applied. Then, by using logistic regression, we tested the accuracy of text data. After testing the model, we created a user interface part of this project; for the user interface part creation, we used a Dash library where the user or client can easily see whether the review is positive or negative. The user interface has two sections; the pie chart: Pie chart section shows the level of positive reviews and percentage or the level of negative reviews and percentage. The second section contains a review textbox where the user types and checks any review. Then, it shows whether the given review about the employee is positive or whether the given review is negative.

Table 5.1   Cronbach's Alpha Value

Reliability Statistics	
Cronbach's Alpha	N (Number of Items)
0.705	20

5.7.1 Reliability

Utilising reliability analysis, we may examine the characteristics of measuring scales and their components. The reliability study provides data on the correlations between the scale's individual items as well as a number of commonly used scale reliability metrics. Cronbach's alpha in our research is 0.705, as shown in Table 5.1, indicating a high level of internal consistency for our scale. Review the probability [if p is 50%, then the model gives its prediction as zero (0); if p is >50%, then the model gives its prediction as one (1)].

5.7.2 Sampling Acceptability

Kaiser–Meyer–Olkin (KMO) is a test that determines how effectively the components make sense of each other in the context of the factors' imperfect relationships. In Table 5.2, KMO values around 1.0 are excellent, whereas those below 0.5 are seen as inappropriate. Most academics currently contest the idea that factor analysis can begin with a KMO of at least 0.80. Our findings in Table 5.2 gave us a KMO esteem of 0.823. It suggests that there is a significant amount of data crossover or a significant degree of imperfect connectivity among the components. Therefore, conducting factor analysis makes sense.

Based on the anti-image metrics, deciding which variables should be left out of the factor analysis is feasible. The numbers in the diagonal are

Table 5.2   Kaiser–Meyer–Olkin Measure of Sampling Adequacy

Kaiser–Meyer–Olkin and Bartlett's Test		
Kaiser–Meyer–Olkin Measure of Sampling Adequacy.		0.823
Bartlett's Test of Sphericity	Approx. Chi-Square	520.728
	df	10
	Sig.	0.000

Table 5.3 Matrix of Anti-Image Correlation

		Artificial Intelligence	Employee Performance	Work Engagement
Anti-image covariance	Artificial intelligence	0.556	–0.136	–0.142
	Employee performance	–0.136	0.363	–0.107
	Work engagement	–0.142	–0.107	0.523
Anti-image correlation	Artificial intelligence	0.869[a]	–0.303	–0.264
	Employee performance	–0.303	0.856[a]	–0.245
	Work engagement	–0.264	–0.245	0.897[a]

used to determine the sample size, and an "a" is superscripted over them. Table 5.3 can be used to evaluate the values. In this instance, the anti-image correlation values vary from 0.856 (employee performance) to 0.897 (work engagement). As a result, all variables can be considered in the factor analysis.

5.7.3 Pearson Correlation

The correlation coefficient of 0.512 in Table 5.4 shows a significant relationship between AI and employee performance. The p-value for this correlation coefficient, which is 0.005, shows how important this relationship is. AI and work engagement have a 0.568 correlation coefficient, showing a moderate association.

5.7.4 Regression

Tables 5.5 and 5.6 show ANOVA summary and coefficient of determination of the variable. The T value for AI is 3.486, and the p-value is 0.001, both of which are lower than 0.05. The T value for AI is 4.236, and the p-value is 0.002, both of which are lower than 0.05. AI, therefore, significantly improves workplace engagement.

Table 5.6 shows the outcome when AI is kept as an independent variable and employee performance and work engagement as a dependent variable. Coefficient of determination of the variable shows after adoption of AI by the organisations, they can focus on data security of the employee's

Table 5.4   Correlation Matrix

		Employee Performance	Work Engagement	Artificial Intelligence
Employee Performance	Pearson correlation	1	0.623**	0.514**
	Sig. (2-tailed)		0	0
	N	200	200	200
Work Engagement	Pearson correlation	0.645**	1	0.643**
	Sig. (2-tailed)	0		0
	N	200	200	200
Artificial Intelligence	Pearson correlation	0.512**	0.676**	1
	Sig. (2-tailed)	0	0	
	N	200	200	200
	N	200	200	200

$^{**}p < .01$

Table 5.5   ANOVA Summary

	Model	Sum of Squares	df	Mean Square	F	Sig.
1	Regression	234.071	4	58.518	72.165	0.000
	Residual	158.124	195	0.811		
	Total	392.195	199			

ANOVA[a]

Table 5.6   Coefficient of Determination of the Variable

Coefficients

	Model	Unstandardised Coefficients B	Std. Error	Standardised Coefficients Beta	t	Sig.
1	(Constant)	−0.757	0.303		−2.498	0.013
	Artificial Intelligence[a]	0.378	0.108	0.255	3.486	0.001[b]

[a] Dependent Variable: Employee Performance and Work Engagement
[b] Predictors: (Constant), Artificial Intelligence

Table 5.7   Model Summary of Variables

Model Summary				
Model	*R*	*R Square*	*Adjusted R Square*	*Std. Error of the Estimate*
1	0.734[a]	0.545	0.512	0.90167

[a] Predictors: (Constant), Artificial Intelligence

performance and work engagement. There are various positive impacts that are depicted in Table 5.6. AI adoption may lead to the employee's autonomy, innovatively, creativity, proper work-life balance along with flexibility. For this, the firms have an option to install a chronological and consecutive AI enactment technique through adopting evidence-based foundations, followed by algorithms and finally adopting the training and development. AI has affected the life styles and work-life balance. The realisation and attainment of AI-driven HR systems rest in the synergetic and associated relationship between the machines of AI and the employees. Regression analysis was used to look at how independent factors affected a dependent variable. Regression analysis also shows the model's adequacy using the R square value. Regression analysis ascertains the degree, which is seen in Table 5.7. According to the coefficient of determination, AI was determined to be responsible for 77.3% of the overall variation in employee performance and work engagement (R square). As a result, we may state that our hypothesis is supported by the data from our study. AI thus has a positive and significant impact on the organisation's job engagement and employee performance.

5.8   Discussions

In the present study, the variation in accuracy for understanding employee sentiments using AI-based text analysis was studied by applying logistic regression techniques. After the model test, we created a file for model saving. Then, finally, a user interface was created. After integrating the user interface with the regression model, the final model that gave the prediction corresponding to each review we have in the data is found. Similarly, results showed that employees who had transactional connections with their employers were more aware of the conditions and amounts of support they might expect. They know their participation will be compensated financially, with no additional obligations or expectations (Klein, Austin, & Cooper, 2008). They remained committed to the company as long as the financial compensation reflected their view of equity and fairness (Rousseau, 1990). An interim HR director, for example, will be devoted to the company that hires her or him for the duration of the contract but will cut links with the organisation and many of the co-workers they worked with after the contract expires.

The study also shows that employees with relational psychological contracts have more robust and long-lasting bonds (Mayer, Davis, & Schoorman, 1995; Rousseau, 1990). There are several facets to the relationship. Relational contract workers affect their surroundings (Saunders & Thornhill, 2003). They influence culture's creation and have the power to alter it. They foster innovation (Chakraborty, Pandey, & Khurana, 2023). They believe they can achieve this because they believe the employer cares about their personal investment in the organisation and their professional growth. The fact that employees with relational contracts have a positive relationship with their employers may not come as a surprise. Additionally, our survey's findings demonstrate that employee engagement directly and favourably impacts worker trust in their organisation. It is a significant discovery since previous research has shown greater trust among employees.

The retention of an employee is dependent on employee engagement. It will become vital on behalf of the organisation to inspire the personnel along the way to get them engaged. Organisations can capitalise on enhancing the variety within the enterprise on the way to enhancing the attrition charge with the assistance of synthetic intelligence. Many companies are going through the demanding situation of retaining variety within the enterprise because it relies on the upkeep of the set of rules that have been designed. Though there are a few demanding situations for using AI, along with facts about privacy, upkeep, skills gaps, upskilling, and economic barriers, the enterprise can efficaciously use AI to increase employee engagement and address variety and fairness worries. AI can also predict mindset behaviour through predictive signs, supporting enterprises in keeping key personnel. The management of skills is a sturdy challenge. HR practices must be monitored cautiously and endorsed for a higher level of aggressiveness to be maintained in an aggressive environment. The numerous guidelines from the secondary facts may be supplied. However, there has to be the proper education and improvement application for the personnel for the robust implementation of the variety within the enterprise and, therefore, regularly taking comments and updates from the numerous teams of employees concerning their pleasure at their place of work to be encouraged. Encouraging and motivating personnel means requiring them to speak about the individuals' troubles and worries inside the enterprise.

5.9 Conclusion

The overview of employee engagement enhancement with the resource of AI identifies that AI-primarily based totally software programmes cannot ably assist control now that it is no longer best to discover the popularity of every employee stage of involvement but additionally count on their attitudes and behaviours through predictive signs, therefore supporting the agency to maintain their key employees. The use of AI is becoming increasingly critical for constructing various workforces. The organisation can correctly use AI to cope with the variety of challenges of the agency, and it may be an utterly compelling device for boosting and keeping variety and fairness within the agency. Future research may be performed with one-of-a-kind geographies and with one-of-a-kind enterprises, including clinics and retail enterprises.

References

Alnuaimi, O. A., Robert, L. P., & Maruping, L. M. (2010). Team size, dispersion, and social loafing in technology supported teams: A theory of moral disengagement perspective. *Journal of Management Information Systems, 27*(1), 203–230.

Cardinal, L. B., Kreutzer, M., & Miller, C. C. (2017). An aspiration view of organisational control research: Re-invigorating empirical work to better meet the challenges of 21st century organisations. *Academy of Management Annals, 21*(4), 559–592.

Carson, C. M. (2005). A historical view of Douglas McGregor's theory Y. *Management Decision, 43*, 450–460.

Chakraborty, S., Pandey, S., & Khurana, A. (2023). Psychological contract types influence on innovative work behaviour: Mediating role of leader–member exchange in service sector during pandemic. *FIIB Business Review.* https://doi.org/10.1177/23197145231156072

Chen, G., & Gogus, C. I. (2008). Motivation in and of work teams: A multilevel perspective. In R. Kanfer, G. Chen, & R. D. Pritchard (Eds.), Work motivation: Past, present, and future (pp. 285–318). New York, NY: Routledge.

Chen, G., & Kanfer, R. (2006). Towards a systems theory of motivated behavior in work teams. In R. M. Kramer, & B. Staw (Eds.), Research in organisational behavior: An annual series of analytical essays and critical reviews (Vol. 27, pp. 223–267). Oxford: Elsevier.

Chen, G., Kanfer, R., DeShon, R. P., Mathieu, J. E., & Kozlowski, S. W. J. (2009). The motivating potential of teams: Test and extension of Chen and Kanfer's (2006) cross-level model of motivation in teams. *Decision Processes, 110*(1), 45–55.

Dirks, K. T., & Ferrin, D. L. (2001). Trust in leadership: Meta-analytic findings and implications for research and practice. *Journal of Applied Psychology, 21*(6), 611–628.

Fay, M. J., & Kline, S. L. (2011). Co-worker relationships and informal communication in high-intensity telecommuting. *Journal of Applied Communication Research, 39*(2), 144–163.

Gallup Report (2017). Gallup State of the global workplace 2017. https://qualityincentivecompany.com/wp-content/uploads/2017/11/Gallup-State-of-the-Global-Workplace-Report-2017_Executive-Summary.pdf

Gerlsbeck, R. (2018). The AI manager. Smith Magazine, Summer Issue. https://smith.queensu.ca/magazine/issues/summer-2018/features/ai-manager.php

Hewitt, L. N. (2001). Volunteer work and well-being. *Journal of Health and Social Behavior, 42*(2), 115–131. https://doi.org/10.2307/3090173

Hu, J., & Liden, R. (2014). Making a difference in the teamwork: Linking team prosocial motivation to team processes and effectiveness. *Academy of Management Journal, 58*, 1102–1127. https://doi.org/10.5465/amj.2012.1142

Hughes, C., Robert, L., Frady, K., & Arroyos, A., (2019). Artificial Intelligence, employee engagement, fairness, and job outcomes. Managing technology and middle- and low-skilled employees (The Changing Context of Managing People) (pp. 61–68). Emerald Publishing Limited.

Kahn, W. A. (1990). Psychological conditions of personal engagement and disengagement at work. *Academy of Management Journal, 33*(4).

Kanfer, R., & Ackerman, P. L. (1989). Motivation and cognitive abilities: An integrative/aptitude-treatment interaction approach to skill acquisition. *Journal of Applied Psychology, 74*(4), 657–690.

Klein, H. J., Austin, J. T., & Cooper, J. T. (2008). Goal choice and decision processes. In R. Kanfer, G. Chen, & R. Pritchard (Eds.), Work motivation: Past, present, and future (pp. 101–150). New York, London: Routledge/Taylor & Francis Group.

Kolbjornsrud, V., Amico, R., & Thomas, R. J. (2016). Article leadership development. *How Artificial Intelligence Will Redefine Management, Harvard Business Review, 2*(1), 3–10.

Kopelman, R. E., Prottas, D. J., & Davis, A. L. (2008). Douglas McGregor's theory x and y: Toward a construct-valid measure. *Journal of Managerial Issues, 20*(2), 255–271.

Luthans, F., & Doh, J. (2012). International management: Culture, strategy, and behaviour. New York: McGraw-Hill.

Maaravi, Y., Heller, B., Shoham, Y., Mohar, S., & Deutsch, B. (2021). Ideation in the digital age: literature review and integrative model for electronic brainstorming. *Review of Management Science, 15*, 1431–1464. https://doi.org/10.1007/s11846-020-00400-5

Mayer, R. C., Davis, J. H., & Schoorman, F. D. (1995). An integrative model of organisational trust. *Academy of Management Review, 20*, 709–734.

McAllister, D. J. (1995). Affect-and cognition-based trust as foundations for interpersonal cooperation in organisations. *Academy of Management Journal, 38*(1), 24–59.

O'Connor, S. (2016, September). When your boss is an algorithm. Financial Times. https://www.ft.com/content/88fdc58e-754f-11e6-b60a-de4532d5ea35

Pandey, S., & Bahukhandi, M. (2022). Applicants' Perception Towards the Application of AI in Recruitment Process. 2022 International Conference on Interdisciplinary Research in Technology and Management, IRTM 2022.

Pandey, S., & Khaskel, P. (2019). Application of AI in human resource management and Gen Y's reaction. *International Journal of Recent Technology and Engineering (IJRTE), 8*(4), 10325–10331.

Pandey, S., Ruhela, V., & Ruhela, S. (2021). Precursors and ramifications of creativity on innovation in product design teams-a study on Indian information technology sector. *Journal of Physics: Conference Series, 1860*(1), 012014.

Parker, S. K., Bindl, U. K., & Strauss, K. (2010). Making Things Happen: A Model of Proactive Motivation. *Journal of Management, 36*, 827–856.

Rothbard, N.P., & Patil S. V. (2011). Being there: Work engagement and positive organizational scholarship. In G. M. Spreitzer, & K. S. Cameron (Eds.), *The Oxford Handbook of Positive Organizational Scholarship* (pp. 57–69). Oxford Library of Psychology.

Rousseau, D. (1990). New hire perceptions of their own and their employer's obligations: A study of psychological contracts. *Journal of Organisational Behaviour, 11*, 389–400.

Saunders, M. N., & Thornhill, A. (2003). Organisational justice, trust and the management of change: An exploration. *Personnel Review, 32*(3), 360–375.

Shuck, B., Adelson, J. L., & Reio, T. G. (2017). The employee engagement scale: Initial evidence for construct validity and implications for theory and practice. *Human Resource Management, 56*, 953–977.

Xiao, B., & Benbasat, I. (2007). E-commerce product recommendation agents: Use, characteristics, and impact. *MIS Quarterly, 31*(1), 137–209.

Chapter 6

Gig Economy: Changing the Dynamics of the Workforce

Manisha Suryawanshi
Modern College of Arts, Science and Commerce (Autonomous), Pune, India

Poonam Ponde
Nowrosjee Wadia College, Pune, India

6.1 Introduction

The gig economy is emerging as transformative work flexibility to individuals, thus shaping modern work arrangements. With the rise in digital platforms and technology, people have more significant opportunities to engage in freelance work, on-demand task-based assignments, etc. There is a considerable need to explore the motivation behind gig work to grasp the social and economic impact on employees and organizations and forecast the opportunities and challenges impacting the policymakers and stakeholders.

The gig economy has created new avenues for income generation; however, there needs to be more concern about employment security, access to various benefits, and leverage for market dynamics (Friedman 2014). The primary drivers are flexibility and autonomy, which attract individuals to gig work.

DOI: 10.4324/9781003372622-6

6.2 The Gig Economy and Its Legal Implications for HR Management

6.2.1 Introduction to Gig Economy

The gig economy has steadily grown in popularity over the past few years. "Gig" refers to short-term contracts or freelance work, often facilitated through digital platforms. The term "gig economy" refers to a labour market where jobs are transient, flexible, and short term. It is also called the "sharing economy" or the "freelance economy." In this economy, people work on a project-by-project basis, frequently working simultaneously for several clients. This work offers workers the flexibility and autonomy while providing companies access to a broader talent pool (Wood, Graham, Lehdonvirta & Hjorth 2019).

6.2.2 Legal Implications for HR Management

The gig economy has created new opportunities and flexible work schedules, but it also presents a few legal challenges for human resource (HR) professionals. HR departments must follow all applicable labour rules and regulations when working with gig workers. This includes appropriately categorizing gig workers as independent contractors or employees, offering required benefits, and addressing any legal risks related to gig labour. Clear policies related to various jobs and roles need to be explicitly defined. It will ease the process of assigning specific jobs to gig workers. Conflict inside a company can become a significant problem without such clarity.

This section will explore some critical legal implications of managing HR in the gig economy.

6.2.2.1 Classification of Gig Workers

Identifying the job status of gig workers is one of the main difficulties of the gig economy. With several high-profile lawsuits contesting the position of gig workers as independent contractors, the classification of gig workers has become contentious in recent years. Gig workers are frequently categorized as independent contractors rather than employees. Because gig workers are classified as independent contractors, employers can only provide them health insurance, overtime pay, and minimum wage benefits. It is unjust to gig workers who may work full-time hours without having the same benefits and protections as employees because it denies them those rights. As independent contractors are not entitled to the same rights and benefits as employees under employment law, this could have serious legal ramifications. Because of this, HR professionals need to be cautious when creating contracts and working arrangements with gig workers to ensure they are classified correctly and that all legal requirements are followed. Workers must be correctly classified by their employers to be eligible for various benefits and protections to ensure compliance with employment laws and avoid legal penalties (Kuhn 2016; Lin 2019).

Ensuring gig workers are accurately classified for tax purposes is another legal difficulty. Employers must submit employee wages to the government tax department and deduct taxes as necessary. Employers are not required to withhold taxes for independent contractors responsible for paying their taxes. HR managers must ensure their company complies with tax rules and regulations to avoid misclassifying employees and incurring hefty fines.

6.2.2.2 Labour Law Compliance

Compliance with wage and hour laws is another legal difficulty the gig economy faces. Many gig workers are paid hourly or on a project-by-project basis; therefore, they might be covered by different laws on minimum wage and overtime than regular employees. Regardless of whether their workers are categorized as employees or independent contractors, employers must abide by several state and federal employment regulations, including wage and hour rules, anti-discrimination laws, and worker's compensation laws.

However, following employment regulations might take much work in the gig economy. Because gig labour is flexible and transient, it can take time for businesses to quantify the hours put in by their freelance workers precisely. Additionally, companies may have less control over gig workers than they do over their full-time employees, which can lead to problems with compliance with the laws. HR professionals are responsible for ensuring that they know relevant wage and hour laws and taking action to ensure compliance for all gig workers (Stewart & Stanford 2017).

6.2.2.3 Employee Benefits

Gig workers are frequently considered independent contractors as opposed to full-time employees. It has ramifications for benefits, including health insurance, retirement plans, workers' compensation, and wage and hour laws. Gig workers may qualify for different uses than employees because many benefits are tied to employment status. Hence, HR professionals must carefully assess the benefits to provide to gig workers following the applicable laws and regulations.

Employers are now beginning to understand the value of providing benefits to their gig workers. For retaining and attracting talent, several businesses have started providing benefits such as health insurance and retirement plans to their gig employees. Offering help to gig workers can be difficult for employers, though, as it can be expensive and complicated to manage benefits for a workforce that is not permanent and constantly changing.

6.2.2.4 Discrimination and Harassment

Every workplace faces ongoing issues regarding discrimination and harassment and the gig economy is no different. Protecting gig workers from harassment and discrimination based on their ethnicity, gender, sexual orientation, or any other trait is the responsibility of HR experts. In the gig economy, workers may receive additional support and security than traditional employees. In cases where they are spread across multiple locations, the issue becomes even more difficult. To ensure that all gig workers are informed of their rights and have access to the proper procedures for reporting any instances of discrimination or harassment, HR professionals must take immediate action.

To conclude, the gig economy poses various legal difficulties for the HR team, from employment status and contractual agreements to pay and hour legislation, worker categorization and benefits, and harassment and discrimination. All gig workers must be treated correctly and follow all legal requirements. Thus, HR professionals must know the pertinent laws and regulations and take appropriate action. HR managers need to stay up to date on the latest legal developments related to the industry.

6.3 Maintaining and Promoting HR Agility in the Gig Economy

A new type of worker who values flexibility over job security has emerged in the gig economy. The traditional employer-employee relationship has changed due to the gig economy, which has made it necessary for organizations to have HR agility. Organizations must develop and maintain HR agility to be competitive in this new work setup. HR agility refers to the ability of an organization to adapt to changes quickly and effectively while ensuring that the staff is motivated and productive.

HR adaptability is essential in the gig economy. Because employees are not constrained by conventional working hours or contracts, businesses must be adaptable in handling HR management. The performance of organizations is more likely to improve if they use an agile approach to HR management, enabling businesses to react swiftly to market and customer needs changes. HR agility may also aid companies in luring top people to the gig economy and keeping them there. It is because gig workers value flexibility and the freedom to choose their hours.

6.3.1 Challenges and Opportunities for HR Agility in the Gig Economy

Managing a diverse and scattered workforce is one of the most significant issues of HRM and its agility in the gig economy. Gig workers may operate from various locations, adhere to multiple work schedules, and be unavailable for assignments. Because of this, businesses must establish new HR procedures that satisfy the requirements of gig employees. However, organizations can benefit from HR agility in the gig economy. Organizations may access a larger talent pool and gain a competitive edge by embracing HR agility. HR agility can also assist businesses in lowering labour expenses and boosting productivity.

This section discusses various strategies organizations can adopt to maintain and promote HR agility, such as developing a flexible workforce, cultivating an agile culture, and using technology to make HR procedures more efficient.

6.3.1.1 Build a Flexible Workforce!

Building a flexible workforce is one of the most important aspects of preserving HR agility in the gig economy. Finding and employing people who can manage a range of jobs and projects requires them to be flexible, adaptive, and adaptable. It also entails creating systems and processes that quickly adapt to shifting corporate demands and labour market conditions.

Focusing on hiring freelancers and contractors with various talents and experiences is one method to create a flexible workforce. By doing this, organizations can ensure that their business has access to a talent pool that may change with the needs of various projects and jobs. Another strategy is to develop a talent network of gig workers who can be called upon as needed for projects. By doing so, there is a guarantee that the organization has access to a pool of qualified personnel who can be rapidly hired for transient projects or to fill skill gaps.

6.3.1.2 Emphasize Flexibility

Organizations must embrace the flexibility of employment as the gig economy is based on a flexible work environment. Employers should offer employees flexible work schedules to successfully juggle work and personal obligations. Telecommuting, job sharing, and flexible hours are all examples of flexible work arrangements. Organizations can recruit and retain talent by offering flexible work options while encouraging work-life balance.

6.3.1.3 Create a Culture of Agility

Developing an agile organizational culture is another crucial aspect of preserving HR agility in the gig economy. It entails creating an atmosphere where employees are urged to be adaptive and flexible and where change is welcomed. Guarantee that workers have the skills they need to succeed in a business environment that is continuously changing (Gaikwad & Pandey 2022). It also requires offering opportunities for ongoing learning and development. Offering regular training and development opportunities that align with the company's objectives and the employee's career aspirations is one method to do this. HR professionals can arrange training programs and resources that help gig employees stay current with the latest technology, tools, and trends in their professions to foster an agile culture. Organizations can create a more motivated and productive workforce that can swiftly adjust to changes by investing in the growth of their employees.

6.3.1.4 Embrace Diversity and Inclusion

Diversity and inclusion are crucial elements of HR agility in the gig economy. Therefore, organizations must actively create a culture of diversity and inclusion to attract and keep great talent from various backgrounds. Organizations can benefit from multiple perspectives and ideas to quickly adjust to changes by cultivating a diverse and inclusive workforce. (Pandey, Ruhela & Ruhela 2021)

6.3.1.5 Embrace Technology

Technology is essential for retaining HR agility and streamlining the HR processes in the gig economy. HR professionals may streamline procedures and workflows, manage remote staff more efficiently, and respond to shifting business needs using digital tools and platforms. Businesses that use technology to automate HR activities, such as hiring and performance monitoring, can work more quickly and effectively. Investing in HR management software, which can automate many of the administrative processes involved in managing a gig workforce, such as tracking hours and payments, managing contracts, and communicating with workers, is one method to use technology. Utilizing digital platforms for talent management is another strategy that can assist HR executives in finding and hiring the best gig workers for jobs or projects. Artificial intelligence (AI)-powered chatbots, for instance, can screen job candidates, thereby freeing HR staff members' time to concentrate on other essential responsibilities. Additionally, payroll and benefits administration can be managed using online platforms, which makes it simpler for employees to access information and administer their benefits (Kamble & Pandey 2022)

6.3.1.6 Create a Feedback Culture

In the gig economy, employees frequently work remotely and occasionally interact with their supervisors face-to-face. Therefore, creating a feedback culture that promotes open communication and regularly provides management with feedback is essential. In order to improve the performance of employees and developing themselves in their positions, managers should offer constructive feedback. A two-way feedback loop that encourages continuous development should be established by encouraging employee feedback to management.

To sum up, firms must maintain and improve HR agility in light of the evolving workplace that the gig economy has created. By embracing technology, encouraging continuous learning, cultivating a feedback culture, focusing on flexibility, and promoting diversity and inclusion, organizations may create a more flexible and resilient workforce. With this strategy, firms may thrive in the gig economy.

6.4 Challenges to Recruiters for Talent Acquisition in the Gig Economy

The gig economy is a rapidly expanding job market segment where people work as independent contractors on a temporary or contractual basis, frequently using internet platforms such as Uber, Airbnb, etc. Because the recruitment process in the gig economy is different from that of traditional employment, it presents additional difficulties for recruiters who must adjust to the unique traits of this workforce. In this section, we will examine the challenges recruiters face in talent acquisition in the gig economy.

6.4.1 Identifying and Attracting Gig Workers

Finding and recruiting gig workers is a massive challenge for recruiters. Gig workers are dispersed over numerous platforms and might not be actively looking for employment, unlike typical hiring procedures when recruiters have a pool of prospects to choose from. Gig workers frequently use several platforms and might not be affiliated with any specific company or business. Therefore, to find talent, recruiters must be innovative. Recruiters must devise creative strategies to connect with prospective prospects, such as establishing a web presence, targeted job advertising, and working with networks that support the gig economy.

6.4.2 Evaluating Skills and Competencies

Many gig workers come from non-traditional backgrounds and need more formal education, which is quite challenging for companies to assess their abilities and competencies (Gaikwad, Pardeshi & Pandey 2022, Sethuraman, Pandey & Pandey 2022). To determine the skills and competencies of gig workers, recruiters must create new metrics that consider their portfolio, project outcomes, and client feedback. They may also employ predictive analytics and skills evaluation tests to determine whether gig workers have what it takes to succeed in the position.

6.4.3 Compliance and Legal Issues

Gig workers are different from regular employees. When hiring gig workers, recruiters must ensure that all employment rules are followed, and regulatory and legal difficulties are dealt with. They must adhere to their gig workers' jurisdiction's governing regulations and labour laws. To avoid legal problems, they must also ensure that the gig workers are correctly designated as independent contractors or employees. To overcome this difficulty, recruiters should consult with legal professionals to ensure they abide by all pertinent rules and laws.

6.4.4 Retaining Gig Workers

Gig workers are not tied to a particular organization or business. Gig workers are highly independent and completely control which gigs they accept and reject. Retaining gig workers is highly challenging for recruiters because gig workers are focused on finding jobs and roles with the highest compensation and flexibility, unlike regular employees who may be loyal to the company. To retain gig workers, recruiters must provide competitive salaries and perks. To keep top talent, recruiters also offer incentives such as bonuses or flexible working conditions. Recruiters must devise plans to keep gig employees by paying them competitively, offering ongoing opportunities for training and growth, and fostering an environment that recognizes their contributions.

6.4.5 Lack of Standardization

The lack of standardized job titles and skill sets in the gig economy presents another difficulty in acquiring personnel. Because gig workers frequently need a regular job title, it can be challenging for recruiters to compare prospects. Furthermore, gig workers could possess a wide variety of non-standard talents. Recruiters can overcome this difficulty by concentrating on a candidate's skills and experience rather than their job title.

6.4.6 Supervising and Managing Remote Teams

Gig workers may operate remotely, making it difficult for recruiters to supervise them successfully. To ensure that gig workers stay on track and accomplish their targets and objectives, recruiters must employ efficient communication tactics, including messaging applications, video conferencing, and project management software (Pandey, Ruhela & Ruhela 2021).

6.4.7 Managing Multiple Platforms

The gig economy's popularity has led to numerous gig platforms, each with its own set of guidelines. Recruiters must first understand these platforms and use these channels to discover the best talent for a specific role (Vallas & Schor 2020). This can be a laborious and time-consuming operation. Recruiters can address this difficulty by using talent management software that integrates with various gig platforms, simplifying the management and tracking of prospective workers.

To conclude, talent acquisition poses challenges for recruiters in the gig economy. Several factors contribute to the difficulty in finding and retaining the right talent. These include needing more standardization in job titles and skill sets, maintaining top talent, adhering to labour laws and regulations, managing various platforms, and managing remote teams (Ruhela and Pandey 2022). Recruiters may overcome these difficulties and identify the best candidates for their organizations by implementing the appropriate tactics and tools, creating a successful talent acquisition strategy, and being creative in their search for talent.

6.5 Incubator and Accelerator

6.5.1 Incubators

The word "incubators" can refer to projects or platforms that offer assistance and resources to freelancers, independent contractors, and gig workers in the gig economy context. These incubators help people start and build their freelancing jobs or gig-based enterprises.

Incubators for the gig economy understand the issues that independent workers confront, such as obtaining clients, marketing their services, handling funds, and developing a viable company model. They aim to bridge the gap by providing gig workers with specialized counselling, training, and networking opportunities.

These incubators could provide various services and resources, such as incubators offering workshops, webinars, and courses to help gig workers improve their skills and expertise (Nair & Blomquist 2019).

Business incubators have received recognition for supporting start-ups and entrepreneurs. They support with environment/physical workspace, access to shared facilities, and offer mentoring services, resources and networking opportunities to help the start-ups to grow. Incubators create an ecosystem that encourages developing innovative ideas, assistance for business planning, exposure to investment networks, market research, legal and accounting support, and job creation, thus leading to economic growth (Gonzalez-Uribe & Leatherbee 2018).

These new ideas are incubated to help new entrepreneurs to convert their ideas into a business model and further into a working business. They help in infrastructure, networking, training and guidance, financial advisory/legal advisory, contacting potential investors, etc.

■ They usually need to provide start-up funding.
■ They are non-profit organizations which academic or government institutions run.
■ In this, the purpose is for the long-term mentorship, working on various ideas and innovations.
■ The main goal is not fundraising. To summarize, incubators play an essential role in economic growth.

6.5.2 Accelerator

It is an initiative designed to support and accelerate the early stage of the company's growth. The accelerator's primary purpose is to reduce the timeline and enhance the chances of development of start-ups by providing them with a supportive ecosystem and structured framework. They work with various start-ups and execute different programs for a fixed duration. The accelerator program addresses key areas such as market validation, business model refinement, product development, sales strategies, financial planning, legal aspects, etc. Accelerators can be specific to the industry, start-ups targeting health care, beauty and wellness, technology, and energy.

■ They help young start-ups and businesses to grow quickly during their starting stages.
■ In short periods, rather than letting them learn by scratch and be successful for-profit.
■ They provide infrastructure, technology and legal guidance, funding in exchange for equity in the company, and networking opportunity.
■ They are usually for-profit ventures.
■ They have monitored timelines for project deliverables and structured guidance.

Therefore, it can be concluded that an accelerator is a program that supports early-stage start-ups, mentoring, networking, and resources and is an integral part of the gig economy.

6.6 Changing the Present and Future Work Equation: A Paradigm Shift

Businesses must find best practices to identify the customer's needs and integrate skill resources from various platforms, data security, intellectual property, etc. In various respects, the gig economy is dramatically transforming the existing and future employment equation. Here are some of the most significant ways that the gig economy is changing the workplace:

Flexibility and autonomy: Grab economy workers have more flexibility and autonomy. Gig workers can work when and how they choose, helping them achieve a better work-life balance. Individuals with caregiving duties, those seeking extra income, or those pursuing personal interests in addition to employment may find this flexibility very advantageous.

Revenue diversification: The gig economy allows individuals to diversify their revenue streams. Workers can take on many gigs or freelance projects instead of relying entirely on regular employment, decreasing reliance on a single employer. It requires the following for effective implementation:

- The organization must validate certificates, internships, expertise, technical skill sets, simulations, etc.
- Management should consider employee feedback, assessment, peer credentials, skill set, people skills, tools, and training courses for gig working.
- Higher management must verify legacy mindset, legality, and complexity in managing skill-based activities and compensation practices.
- It should create a human-centric work model for holistic well-being, including collaboration, learning, and behavioural skills.
- Future skills like teamwork, creativity, critical thinking, good attitude and aptitude, problem-solving ability, and innovative ideas must be highlighted, including becoming more adaptable and adjusting to new environments.
- Organizations must look forward to current techno-savvy gig workers having leadership, social influence, problem-solving ability, digital literacy, initiative, technology design, design thinking, usage of emerging trends, AI, etc.
- There must be a focus on how to design job roles, use technology to track employee skills, fit the right people for various functions, and provide rewards/bonuses to the gig workers.
- Manage the workforce, and focus on optimized scheduling to boost productivity, efficiency, and client satisfaction.

6.7 Promoting Flexibility and Managing People in Client Centres

Businesses using the gig economy model must pay attention to the following issues in order to provide effective services to their clients:

- Training employees to prepare their schedules, set timelines, and understand priorities.
- Understanding the people from the client centre and other stakeholders.
- Encourage open communication and implementation of the agile model in client centres.
- Participation in voluntary activities.
- Develop flexibility in work policy at all levels to increase customer engagement.
- Design the job to clarify each team member's role clearly and show the path to understanding the contribution of each member's performance on the overall project.
- Demonstrate consistent leadership, giving timely feedback, understanding challenges, overcoming them, and resolving conflicts.
- Manage the team of clients by respecting timelines, educating the clients, involving them in various processes, and offering amazing service.
- Organizations can use client management tools such as Monday.com, AllClients, Zoho, Zendesk HubSpot, etc., for effective functioning.

6.8 Policy Development for Hybrid Employee

Many companies are adopting hybrid work policies, which develop trust between employers and employees, leading to a new work culture.

- In a hybrid work model, companies can define the policies for employees regarding their timely deliverables, meeting deadlines of projects, producing desired output, maintaining good rapport with the client, etc.
- Employees get the flexibility to work from home or work from the office.
- Employees must be awarded a performance bonus, better work-life balance, training sessions on desired technologies, etc.
- Allowances can be provided to employees for internet, required furniture, and other bonuses depending on their performance.

- Employee productivity can be increased by avoiding workplace distractions, lessening commute time, and maintaining work-life balance.
- Organizations can provide GYM membership, yoga and fitness classes, travel allowances if employees have to travel abroad, free consultation for tax returns, etc.
- Organizations should encourage family and team outings, team open houses, family day celebrations and team lunches and gatherings for team development, and interpersonal effectiveness.
- A solid platform and ecosystem must be created and outfitted for hybrid communication with the appropriate tools and technologies.
- Employees should be given proper guidelines for working remotely from the office, ensuring connectivity among remote teams, clients, and employers.
- Organizations must explain to their employees the proper use of internet resources, firewalls, antivirus updates, and other security measures working remotely or in hybrid mode.
- Employees who work from home have fewer social connections with their teams, necessitating the acquisition of office culture experience. Employees prefer interacting with their seniors to gain hands-on experience, develop teams, and engage with coworkers and other stakeholders. As a result, a company need to work on growth strategy for a hybrid work culture experience.

6.9 Employers' Lookout

Because of the gig economy, freelancers can earn money by doing flexible and remote assignments, including clients that care more about the quality of the work than the sort of credentials the freelancer possesses. Millennial workers primarily utilize it to supplement their income and appreciate the freedom and control it provides over their work schedule. It is a challenge for employers to get gig workers with the required skills and competencies since investing time and money in developing competencies in gig workers is a liability for them. Following are the employers' lookout for gig workers:

- Attract and retain diverse talent, thus having a wider talent pool team of consultants, freelancers, etc.

- Increasing innovation and creativity at the workplace for improved productivity with gig workers.
- Working policy for the gig workers as many freelancers are not keen to develop themselves and need to be more flexible in working.
- Reduce office infrastructure costs, hospitality services, etc.
- Provide employees with increased flexibility with guidelines on do's and don'ts for working from the office/working from home.
- Identify and measure critical success and failure factors, forecasting the scope for improvisation.
- Plan for various iterations, verification, and validation of performances.
- Respect and motivate employees' sentiments and feedback for company growth structure improvements.

To summarize, a gig economy with greater flexibility and transparency is the future, thus changing present and future work equations. It can be helpful for the people who are looking for a little more money. However, it has significant disadvantages for those seeking a steady, predictable income and some protection from the ups and downs of the market, as well as employers seeking a dependable, collaborative workforce. As the gig economy evolves, it becomes evident that every trend has its boundaries. Nonetheless, with the rise of start-ups that rely on an increasing supply of freelance gig workers, there is a growing need to understand the nature of the gig economy and the workers who support it, as well as to learn how to develop HR policies, law and the company as a whole to recognize its full potential. The typical gig worker does not seek to escape traditional employer responsibilities. That is already in place. They want to hold their employer accountable to them. For employers, the gig economy is essentially a win-win situation. Businesses can swiftly contract with professionals for specific projects without incurring overhead costs such as office space, training, and perks.

References

Friedman, G. (2014). Workers without employers: shadow corporations and the rise of the gig economy. Review of Keynesian Economics, 2(2), 171–188.

Gaikwad, H. V., Pardeshi, A. S., & Pandey, S. (2022). Surmounting the five-headed dragon: Best practices of technical institutes in rural Maharashtra – success of the institution in online education. EdTech Economy and the Transformation of Education, pp. 157–167, DOI: 10.4018/978-1-7998-8904-5.ch009.

Gaikwad, P., & Pandey, S. (2022). A review on Special Skill Sets from Industry 4.0 Perspective. Proceedings – 2022 2nd International Conference on Electronic and Electrical Engineering and Intelligent System, ICE3IS, 276–281.

Gonzalez-Uribe, J., & Leatherbee, M. (2018). The effects of business accelerators on venture performance: evidence from Start-Up Chile. The Review of Financial Studies, 31(4), 1566–1603.

Kamble, S., & Pandey, S. (2022). Perception gap analysis of "employability" amongst academia, IT-industry and fresh engineering graduates. ECS Transactions, 107(1), 10857–10864.

Kuhn, K. M. (2016). The rise of the "gig economy" and implications for understanding work and workers. Industrial and Organizational Psychology, 9(1), 157–162.

Lin, L.-H. (2019). Technology interdependence and entry modes of the Taiwanese technological multinational companies: moderating effects of political instability, technological uncertainty, and Confucian dynamism. Technology Analysis & Strategic Management, 31(6), 707–719.

Nair, S., & Blomquist, T. (2019). Failure prevention and management in business incubation: practices towards a scalable business model. Technology Analysis & Strategic Management, 31(3), 266–278.

Pandey, S., Ruhela, V., & Ruhela, S. (2021). Precursors and ramifications of creativity on innovation in product design teams – a study on Indian information technology sector. Journal of Physics: Conference Series, 1860(1), 012014.

Ruhela, V., & Pandey, S. (2022). Emotional intelligence, conflict management styles and innovative work behaviour – a study on Indian employees. International Journal of Early Childhood Special Education, 14(4), 2678–2684.

Sethuraman, M., Pandey, S., & Pandey, R. (2022). Career in textile museum. Handbook of museum textiles. Conservation and Cultural Research, I, 355–381.

Stewart, A., & Stanford, J. (2017). Regulating work in the gig economy: what are the options? The Economic and Labour Relations Review, 28(3), 420–437.

Vallas, S., & Schor, J. B. (2020). What do platforms do? Understanding the gig economy. Annual Review of Sociology, 46, 273–294.

Wood, A. J., Graham, M., Lehdonvirta, V., & Hjorth, I. (2019). Good gig, bad gig: autonomy and algorithmic control in the global gig economy. Work, Employment and Society, 33(1), 56–75.

Chapter 7

Re-Imaging Human Resource Strategic Approaches: Adoption of Metaverse

Sankar Mukherjee
GIBS Business School, Bangalore, India

Gaurav Gupta
Galgotias University, Greater Noida, India

7.1 Introduction

"Meta" is a word in the English dictionary to signify the change of position and state. The verse is a rhythmic approach to arranging the lines to connect the dots of the meaning of the words. In the same way, metaverse alters the Internet's fundamental principles for the future. It is the next generation of the Internet as envisioned by advanced technology. Metaverse will create a new digital environment connecting all the digital platforms seamlessly under one umbrella, creating a universal digital landscape. The first time the word "metaverse" was used in a science-fiction book called "Snow Crash," which came out in 1992. The words "meta" and "universe" were put together to make the word "metaverse," in which characters are said to be living an alternative life (Stephenson, 2003). Metaverse could change human behaviour in digital space with the interface with technology shortly. Moreover, it can radically shift technology transformation by connecting.

Even the idea and philosophy behind the metaverse have been used since then, mostly in films and video games. For example, one theory says that games

DOI: 10.4324/9781003372622-7

like Roblox, Minecraft, and Fortnite, where players meet in 2D environments and play with each other, are driven by a basic metaverse. Within the metaverse, netizens may perform all online activities under one roof currently being completed with different digital points like websites, apps, social media, etc. The dream of password-free access or a singular password regime will unfold with the introduction of the metaverse's new digital experience.

7.2 Metaverse: The Mechanism

What is above the Internet world? The metaverse is considered a future world. If we told you that you are present in Delhi and at the same time you are partying with your friends in Goa, or you are seen with your friends in your house as well, would you believe this? No, it is not even a matter of belief because it is impossible to happen, but believe me, it will happen in the future. This is the core principle of the metaverse: to make you present in a new digital avatar around the digital universe. An imaginary world while sitting at home, you will roam freely into this virtual world with the help of virtual reality (VR) handsets. You can go shopping in this world, but you have to use cryptocurrency. You can play any type of game and make new friends, which means you can do all that you are currently doing in this world. Not only this but you will also be given a different name in this world.

■ A digital environment that is 360 degrees and blends the real and virtual worlds
■ A digital space with a full-fledged economy where financial deals can be made
■ Interoperability: the ability and usefulness to move from one metaverse to another

The metaverse forms an alternative world where individuals portray themselves as digital avatars and perform sets of activities irrespective of their geographical locations.

7.3 Metaverse Meets Digital Economy

Integrating different platforms across multiple pockets of devices can create a holistic digital ecosystem. Currently, augmented reality (AR) and VR-propelled handsets are the connecting devices. But, the array of digital devices such as smartwatches, smartphones, laptops, personal computers, gaming consoles, and tablets are ready to plug in connection with the metaverse.

Virtual worlds that are almost identical to our natural world, like offices, shopping malls, and organisations, will change the entire landscape of the digital economy. A significant investment in digital devices and the Internet of things (IoTs) is transforming day to day experience of life.

This technology is going to unfold to bring radical change into the digital ecosystem. Meta has already put $10 billion into its work on the metaverse. In 2014, it bought the VR company Oculus Vision Tech. A whopping capital investment is paving the way for creating a circular economy by connecting with the digital economy (Kraus, Filser, and Puumalainen, 2020).

7.4 Ownership of the Metaverse

There is no singular ownership in this technology, but multiple technological giants are in the fray to provide the service of a portal (gateway) to the metaverse. Each of the giants is competing to build up the infrastructure that creates a platform to facilitate the access point. Facebook has changed its name to Meta. In this regard, Facebook CEO Mark Zuckerberg has also said that he is changing the network's name so that he can take people to the world of the network reported Reuters 2021. In preparation for the metaverse, companies like Walmart and Nike are busy filing for trademark protection and copyright on virtual versions of their goods.

7.5 Metaverse Makes the Difference in Business: A Value Creation Mechanism

The future and the advancement of technology depend on its application and subsequent adoption. The following features of the metaverse will take the business operation to a new scale. The metaverse will create a big canopy under which business operations will change their nature. Although most people worldwide have not even heard of the word metaverse, it has abundant potential to grow. A recent study suggests that 65% of people use the Metaverse headset for at least one hour a day for work, shopping, connecting on social media, chatting, and watching videos through VR and AR (Times of India (TOI), July 2022). Another research report revealed that it could potentially create a whopping value of $5 trillion in the business economy. More than $120 billion in capital has been pumped into the global economy through the project's implementation until 2022. Seventy-nine per cent of used and active consumers in the metaverse have made a purchase, and more than 15% of corporate revenue is expected to be generated through the metaverse application (McKinsey and Company, 2023). So, the metaverse is an inseparable and indispensable entity for the business to come due to benefits it has to offer (Charlton, 2022).

7.6 Business Interface with the Metaverse: across Different Functions 3D AVATAR

A new consumer experience will be ascertained through 3D technology in the virtual environment. Every user will have a digital identity to experience the different forms of operation of the respective organisation. Brand management, product features, promotional campaigns, logistic and supply chain management, manufacturing function, distribution, cost management, behavioural finance, recruitment and retention, and understanding organisational behaviour are a few.

7.7 Manufacturing Industry

With the metaverse in play, it has the most significant impact on the manufacturing industry. Under product management, multiple stages are underway before products are finally commercialised. Procurement of raw materials, prototyping, and the test phase consume the most time and have minor end-user engagement. Metaverse will further accelerate the process of these stages by verifying stages like trial production testing, operation management, marketing, etc., through engagement with the virtual community.

7.8 Brand Management

With the rise of Q-commerce and e-commerce, the metaverse will offer a new shopping experience through meaningful interaction with the virtual community. Through the AR platform, the metaverse can provide unique experiences to its customer base. Immersive shopping experiences are another area where the metaverse can enhance engagement and consumer delight by connecting with brand resonance (Dincelli and Yayla, 2022). Brand loyalty will enhance with interaction and engagement in the virtual environment.

7.9 Technology Upgradation under Integration

Social media interaction, artificial intelligence (AI), the Internet of Things (IoTs), blockchain, natural language processing, and image processing will transform the user experience to make the metaverse more adaptive for modern-day users. All the technologies will integrate into one virtual environment to exchange mutual benefits.

7.10 Experience the Tools of Gamification

Customer engagement will be intensified with the product and service under the behavioural intentions of pre-purchase and post-purchase. Brand awareness and brand resonance will reach a new scale under gamification tools.

7.11 Redefined the Area of Cyber Security

Cyber security is the primary concern for technological advancement; technology implementation at the ground and grassroots levels demands high data protection. Metaverse is a game changer in these areas by providing data security backed by blockchain under the asset's security management (Gadekallu et al., 2022). Business operations can reach into the nooks and crannies to build trust in data protection among users and foster business operations.

7.12 A Paradigm Shift in Human Resource Management: The Role of the WEB 3.0 Metaverse

The multi-dimensional challenge of today's HR function makes human capital management more challenging and robust. A human asset is considered moving capital. The doyen of the Indian software industry, Mr. N.R. Murthy, says that it is the most vulnerable asset as it moves from one place to another. It is not appropriate to make people wait for their benefits (PTI 2023). Hence, the dynamic nature of managing human resources has constantly changed. The adoption of new technology has given a new dimension to HR functions. From talent acquisition to talent retention, the nature of Human management functions is complex. Metaverse will bring radical changes into every domain of HR functions as a futurist approach to human resource management (HRM). So, the opportunity is abundant in strategic human resource management (SHRM). Adopting technology through the system of electronic human resource management (E-HRM) is taking a very prominent place in today's HR operations. The policy, process, and practice adopted under SHRM connect with web-based channels. HR policy has become more transparent with the integration of technology into the various forms of HR functions.

Applying the new version of the World Wide Web (Web 3.0) metaverse will take the different human resource areas into a new virtual HR platform. Virtual HR has become a reality with the application of metaverse technology.

7.13 HR in the Metaverse: A New Space in the Virtual World

7.13.1 Best Experience for Potential Employees: A Redefined Approach to Talent Acquisition

Talent acquisition is one of the most sought-after HRM practices. Over time, human resource operations have made several changes by adopting many strategies to attract and acquire the best talent for the organisation. But the gap remains. Interaction in virtual space through the metaverse application under the innovation of VR and AR will now provide a 360-degree experience to potential employees and recruiters to select the right company and the right candidate. The incumbent is getting more insightful information about organisational behaviour and culture by exchanging dialogue in the virtual environment.

7.13.2 Work-Life Balance: A Way of Quadrilateral Shift under the Application of Metaverse

Work-life balance through working from home has become a buzzword in SHRM. Many large organisations are exploring different ways to provide the best solution for adopting work-life balance. COVID-19 makes it more significant and draws a new dimension called a hybrid work structure with meetings and interaction among employees under a technology platform. Remote work collaboration, where colleagues in an organisation can interact and share dialogue seamlessly, is the new definition of work-life balance. Metaverse can play a poignant role in connecting and collaborating among all the employees in a virtual environment to increase productivity in an inclusive work environment.

7.13.3 Talent Nurture: Foster a Faster Learning Experience through the Metaverse

Immersive training experiences are the most sought-after approaches in training now. The conventional path of training and learning has changed over time. It is an experiential training method that applies VR to showcase real-world scenarios through simulation and gamification. Immersive training approaches are the most effective tools for gaining hands-on training experience. Metaverse is the new avatar in this area to provide a tailor-made solution for specific job-related training through VR handsets and glasses. Under the integration of the metaverse, AR, VR, and AI are creating experiential learning to transport employees into a new learning environment where they are more engaged and develop requisite skills at a deeper level than previously possible. AI-based games are getting popularity in talent market (Pandey and Bahukhandi, 2022).

7.13.4 HR Automation and Employee Engagement: The Metaverse Way

The thumb rule of HRM is to look after human capital. But as per recent research, almost 40% of HR leaders in large organisations complain that they are more engaged with paperwork than nurturing human capital. The Key Responsible Authorities (KRAs) are dominated by more paperwork and administrative work. So, the focus shift has moved from developing work-friendly policies to paper-friendly policies. Hence, transformation is the need of the hour for people. Analytics in performance management, workforce planning, employee engagement, making promotions, and assessing performance appraisal management are the key areas where the metaverse can play a pivotal role in capturing data and making data-driven analytical decisions (World Economic Forum, 2023).

7.13.5 Compliance Automation: A Path of Change under the Metaverse

There is a big makeover under recruitment and background verification (BGV) compliance in the hiring procedure. Automation through technology adoption in the new, unexplored territory where the metaverse can play an intuitive role by facilitating data sharing among organisations and providing data security protection mechanisms under blockchain technology.

7.14 Conclusion

Metaverse is the new avatar for the management operation. HRM will gain substantially through applying and adapting the metaverse across the sector. The significant challenges lie in the cost implications and adopting the culture of embracing the technology at the grassroots level. Data security and privacy issues are another area to be deeply explored. The cost of equipment and mass-scale rollout is another uphill task for organisations to make successful. The policy framework in the place of law and regulation has yet to be made clear. Financial fraud and counterfeit products can occur in a virtual environment. So, the implication of law and a regulatory framework need to be imposed in order to protect data from snooping and make the metaverse universally accessible to all for the holistic development of the business economy.

References

Charlton, E. (2022). 71% of executives say the metaverse will be good for business. Here's why. World Economic, 198.

Dincelli, E., and Yayla, A. (2022). Immersive virtual reality in the age of the metaverse: a hybrid-narrative review based on the technology affordance perspective. Journal of Strategic Information Systems, 31(2).

Gadekallu, T.R., Huynh-The, T., Wang, W., Yenduri, G., Ranaweera, P.S., Pham, Q., Costa, D.B., and Liyanage, M. (2022). Blockchain for the Metaverse: A Review. *ArXiv, abs/2203.09738*. Available from: https://doi.org/10.48550/arXiv.2203.09738.

Kraus, S., Filser, M., Puumalainen, K., Kailer, N., and Thurner, S. (2020). Business model innovation: a systematic literature review, International Journal of Innovation and Technology Management, 17(6), 1–20.

Mckinsey and Company. (2023). Value creation in the metaverse. https://www.mckinsey.com/capabilities/growth-marketing-and-sales/our-insights/value-creation-in-the-metaverse

Pandey, S., and Bahukhandi, M. (2022). Applicants' perception towards the application of AI in recruitment process. 2022 International Conference on Interdisciplinary Research in Technology and Management, IRTM 2022.

PTI. (2023). www.outlookindia.com/business/delhi-is-one-city-where-indiscipline-is-the-highest-n-r-narayana-murthy-news-264044

Stephenson, N. (2003). Snow crash: a novel. Spectra.

Thomson Reuters (2021). Facebook Changes Name to Meta, CEO Mark Zuckerberg Says Rebranding Reflects Investment in 'Metaverse'.

Times of India (TOI). (July 2022). The era of 2022: future of fitness in the metaverse.

World Economic Forum. (2023) What trends will define world of work in 2023. www.weforum.org/agenda/2023/01/trends-world-of-work-in-2023-leaders/?_

Chapter 8

Blockchain Technology in HR Processes

Kuldeep Singh Kaswan and Sumit Kumar Dhanda
Galgotias University, Greater Noida, India

Jagjit Singh Dhatterwal
Koneru Lakshmaiah Education Foundation, Vaddeswaram, India

Balamurugan Balusamy
Shiv Nadar University, Greater Noida, India

8.1 Introduction

Human resource management (HRM) is a field that, if effectively managed, can be a strategic advantage for businesses, and forward-thinking company executives widely acknowledge this fact. Spence (2018) stressed the importance of investing in employee development and actively finding and hiring the best staff. The complexity of HR is growing as businesses of all sizes rely more and more on temporary workers and other non-standard forms of employment. Temporary workers, for instance, may band together for the duration of a single project, only to disperse and be reassembled later for work on other projects in completely different environments and for entirely different employers. Finding the right talent, having them agree to particular terms/conditions, drafting temporary contracts, and legally screening for any disinformation is time-consuming and hazardous, but this method of gathering and distributing talent is deemed more successful (Kaswan, Dhatterwal, and Kumar, 2021).

DOI: 10.4324/9781003372622-8

Today, in the information age, HR professionals face more complex problems than ever before. HR spends much effort, for instance, cross-referencing and screening applicants, running validation tests, and authenticating data to reduce the possibility of poor hiring. A recruiter's primary responsibility is to establish connections between candidates' profiles and numerous data sources, including but not limited to direct applications, recruitment agencies, and social networking sites. Therefore, reviewing applications takes a lot of effort and time. We have already discussed how the blockchain system will have far-reaching and comprehensive implications for HR procedures. Employers and businesses may use blockchain network solutions by employing intelligent contracts to deal with different HR issues across several roles, such as profile verification, performance evaluation, credential verification, and data management. Since blockchain transactions are permanent and secure, potential employers may confidently begin vetting candidates by verifying their credentials and past achievements in the field. Thanks to the blockchain ledger's immutability and decentralized nature, applicants may confidently highlight their unique talents and accomplishments irrespective of a simple reference letter (Elayan, 2021).

8.2 Protection of Cloud Computing Environment in HR Activities

It is critical to provide trustworthy transaction security and ways to verify the origin of a value exchange to prevent fraud, hacking, and ransomware in today's Internet and cloud computing environments. Trustworthy, long-lasting networks are essential to making this work. As a trustworthy system where data is verifiable, irreversible, and unchangeable, blockchain technology may be used to verify the veracity of the information handled daily. It is a database that grows over time, including a digital copy of all the transactions that have ever been completed. Additionally, blockchain's chronological storage of transactions is a benefit (Fachrunnisa and Hussain, 2020). The blockchain infrastructure is based on the following distinctive features. The first is decentralization, which occurs when the system successfully distributes trust and ensures a smooth flow of information while restricting interactions between intermediaries. The data is only added to the blockchain ledger after getting approval from most of the network and adequate confirmation that the cryptographically sent information is legitimate (Dhatterwal et al., 2022a). Consistency is also a defining feature of the system. Each piece of information sent over the network must be authenticated and documented, making it exceedingly unlikely that a transaction would be interrupted while in progress. The blockchain ledger is not administered by a single organization (a person, corporation, or government) but rather by all network computers participating worldwide. Thus, this process shows that two or more parties do not require any third-party certifying authority to validate the legitimacy of transactions or documents before exchanging data. Since the technology eliminates the requirement for a third party's services throughout the agreement and transaction processes, it may result in significant cost savings (Fremont and Jonathan, 2018).

Furthermore, blockchains are immutable digital ledgers that are stored and shared throughout a network, eliminating the need for a single authority to verify transactions. In its most basic version, blockchain technology enables a community of users to record transactions in a distributed ledger accessible only to the community members and once recorded; these transactions cannot be undone. A distributed blockchain is a digital ledger that stores blocks of cryptographically signed transactions (Berwal, Dhatterwal, Kaswan, and Kant, 2022). Each block is made unchangeable by a cryptographic connection to the one before it when verification and conclusions have been reached. It becomes exceedingly difficult to change the older blocks of information when new blocks of information are put into the system, generating tamper resistance. In this system, many copies of the ledger are distributed over the network so that whenever a new block of data is added, it is immediately available everywhere. In the event of a disagreement arising from that procedure, the system will automatically handle it as per the predetermined rules established at the time the system was created (Lukić, Salkić, and Ostojić, 2018).

Multiple blockchain architectures have been considered in prior studies. There are several blockchains, but the most prominent are public, private, and Consortium. With a Public blockchain, anybody may oversee transparent transactions on the network without revealing their identity. It is entirely decentralized and is most often used based on user consensus. For example, Bitcoin uses a similar pattern.

On the other hand, it is vulnerable to cyber assaults since a hacker may conceivably replicate and ultimately chain all the new information blocks without the users' knowledge, although users of a Private blockchain recognize all the transactions as data stored on the network is kept secret from the public. More specifically, a user can neither add nor see any data stored in the Blockchain network unless they have been granted access to the system by the existing members (Lukić, Salkić, and Ostojić, 2018). Most organizations typically use such processes with well-defined roles for all the blockchain enterprise's stakeholders. Finally, a Consortium blockchain combines public and private blockchains into a single system. When adopting this strategy, businesses may create their blockchain network to distribute data to the Consortium's user base, including financial institutions, other businesses, or even governments (Makridakis and Christodoulou, 2019).

8.3 Trust Relations and Confidentiality

Even while blockchain has permeated many facets of our business and redefined how we engage, manage, execute, and verify, its early impact was seen primarily in the sectors related to financial markets and transactions. Slowly but surely, its pervasive and significant effect on HR procedures in the workplace has made it a valued tool (Kaswan, Dhatterwal, Kumar, and Lal, 2022).

As was previously discussed, this technology makes it possible to create a trustless and self-driving economic system. This novel introduction to the digitalization of trust and confidence is the beginning of a transformative effect on HRM in the workplace. Peer-to-peer communication made possible by blockchain technology simplifies and speeds up the employment process by connecting employers directly with competent applicants while simultaneously cutting costs by eliminating the need for mediators. Therefore, thanks to blockchain technology, job seekers may securely communicate with recruiters directly. Furthermore, using a blockchain network's information exchange procedure, a candidate's history may be confirmed in an immutable and truthful manner. Since no intermediaries are needed in a blockchain transaction, the inherent trust between buyers and sellers is strengthened. In the end, it is understood that this technology can lessen the burden on businesses and boost the efficiency of transactions by decreasing the number of intermediaries, in addition to the obvious advantage of making it easier to form connections between people (Kaswan, Dhatterwal, Sood, and Balusamy, 2022).

This means that a combination of transparency and privacy in its service may help establish consumers' trust in the technology. As the network permits contact with several entities, it is natural for HR practices relating to hiring to shift from placing faith in a single person or organization to trusting the population as a whole (Fremont and Jonathan, 2018). As a result, this cutting-edge technology will significantly impact establishing a culture of openness and trust between management and staff.

8.4 Technological Innovations in HR Activities

Thus, it is evident that these rapidly evolving technological innovations have launched and will continue to bring about a wide range of cutting-edge improvements in the HR sector. Keeping data secure and private is at the heart of HR procedures, and blockchain technology is a good match for HR since HR has to handle sensitive information about their employees and the business (Nascimento et al., 2019).

One of the significant advantages of the blockchain network is that it allows for the careful monitoring and validation of data storage. In the blockchain Network, records such as financial transactions, contracts, and ownership transfers are publicly linked to the time and date when they were created because of the system's time-stamping capabilities. Each party may easily and quickly see who started a transaction and when or verify that specific data existed on a certain date. Blockchain uses public-private key cryptography to assure data authenticity and transparency (Neiheiser and Inácio, 2019). It is predicated on the fact that people on a network may freely exchange public keys while keeping their identities secret via private keys. A private encrypted communication or transaction is inaccessible to anybody who does not also possess the appropriate public key that the sender provided. However, if the data is encrypted using a private key, only the receiver can decode it.

In legal agreements, "smart contracts" are a kind of computer code that may carry out the terms of transactions between two parties without needing a third party to mediate the agreement. These contracts were designed so that they could call blockchain-based programming that could do anything. This paves the way for developing escrow arrangements that function without third-party mediators (Onik, Miraz, and Kim, 2018). When specific criteria are met, a contract is automatically enforced across all nodes on a blockchain. HR departments often complain that they need more information from temporary or permanent candidates due to a lack of openness. Job seekers may find it challenging to adhere to this procedure when they have yet to learn where their application is or whether fair, non-discriminatory processes have been applied to screen their applications. However, using blockchain technology and smart contracts might make the employment agreement process open and decentralized (Pinna and Ibba, 2017).

The current HR fad involves temporary work contracts, which are crucial in the global economy and society. Rising worldwide competition, sluggish economic development, and rising unemployment have all contributed to a rise in non-standard contractual arrangements and increased demand for flexible work schedules inside organizations. Competition between businesses on a global scale may reveal emerging issues and encourage adaptation to new circumstances. Thus, temporary work may be an essential competitive strategy on businesses. However, there are drawbacks to temporary work that should be considered (Salleh and Radzi, 2019). These include the absence of protections for workers, lower pay, a lack of opportunities for vocational training owing to time constraints, and, ultimately, diminished career advancement and social security benefits. The rising worries about contract labour may be alleviated using a blockchain network, guaranteeing dependability, trust, and openness. Every bit of data entered into the system is recorded in chronological order and broadcasted wherever it is used, thanks to the digital ledger that stores and eliminates all of the data (Samani et al., 2012).

8.5 Law and Authentication in Blockchain Technology

Also, blockchain enables the development of legally compliant contracts that protect employers and employees. Accordingly, the authority may check these smart contracts for conformity anytime it sees fit. Pinna and Ibba (2017) unveiled the Decentralized Employment System (D-ES), a blockchain-based system designed to help businesses draft short-term contracts that are both legally binding and respectful of the rights of the parties engaged in the transaction. The D-ES does this via smart contracts, which enable the system to automatically analyse any agreement and data acquired between the employer and employee and generate the contract. Thus, it oversees, regulates, and checks on the proper carrying out of a labour agreement. As a result, the time and effort spent on drafting contracts are reduced, accuracy is improved, and legal requirements are strictly enforced, all while providing more security for the workers. A well-implemented blockchain system may help protect sensitive employee data like payroll, banking, health information, performance reviews, expense claims, and disciplinary records from external hackers (Sarda and Chowdhury, 2018).

8.6 Security, Fraud Prevention and Productivity Gains

Data authenticity in personnel acquisition directly affects HRM's efficiency, morale, and output. Some applicants may try to hide adverse outcomes or provide false information to recruiters throughout the hiring process. Many applicants include false information on their resumes, including fake training and graduation certificates, endorsements, prizes, promotions, etc. According to "The Hidden Risks of Recruitment" (2017) by Walker, HR professionals are under extra time demands as their bosses expect a more strategic HR role in maintaining and improving HR processes throughout the organization. The HR department has high expectations, including the ability to hire the finest people and provide them with a pleasant place to work. However, only a minority of HR divisions believe they have enough resources to meet these needs. HR departments have identified many things that could improve the background-checking of their newly hired. These voids put businesses in danger of employing ineffective workers, leading to sluggish productivity, shoddy work, the need for extra help from co-workers, unhappy customers, poor morale, and a tarnished brand (Sauppé and Mutlu, 2015).

HR professionals are exposed to much paperwork throughout the hiring process, some of which may include fraudulent information provided by applicants. HR firms are often used by businesses to verify the claims of candidates to reduce the legal and financial risks associated with hiring people who have lied about their employment history, education, and other qualifications. However, in addition to being time-consuming and expensive, this verification procedure exposes the danger of being partnered with a dishonest and unreliable third-party HR firm that does not protect the privacy of its clients. Many small- and medium-sized businesses (SMBs) skip the verification of job applicants' identities irrespective of knowing the importance of it. The studies have shown the importance of blockchain technology to HR departments for saving costs for verified information about job applicants. It is well-established that privacy and reliability are the most crucial and appealing factors to HR professionals. Thus, establishing trust in shared data becomes crucial (Dhatterwal, Kaswan, and Ojha, 2022b).

8.7 Blockchain-Based Monitoring Surveillance

With the encrypted nature of its internal communications, blockchain technology also provides more protection for particularly sensitive data, such as financial transactions. Blockchain's main strength is that it is not just a platform for settling financial transactions but also a decentralized, unalterable, vital platform for any data that has to be updated and sent across a server. Because of this unique feature, the technology is well-suited for processing and certifying any data, transaction, work credential, or confidential record or document. Several advantages exist for employees who have their HR information stored digitally. For instance, only the employee's present company has the right to add new information to the network after their permission. Also, neither the employee's current nor previous employers will have any information on when and how often or by whom potential employers view their records.

No changes may be made once an employee's record has been created and verified for inclusion in the system. Instead, new information and achievements will be updated in chronological chunks as needed by each current employer. Employees may keep an accurate and up-to-date record of their employment history while also making it easy to present the papers they have chosen to prospective employers or recruitment firms. Since everything is recorded digitally with no paper trail necessary, it was also stated that the enhanced blockchain technology makes employment data conveniently accessible and organized, removing the possibility of fraud when evaluating a candidate's record. Gains in productivity may be realized as a consequence of using an HR blockchain network, as employees will be better able to apply their knowledge and the outcomes of their efforts to their jobs.

As reported by "The Australian Financial Review," the average amount of time it took to fill a position in Australia in 2015 was 68 days, a 50% increase from 2010. The most time-consuming and challenging part of the recruiting process is verifying the accuracy of the candidate's profile (historical background). This requires contacting the candidate's previous employers to collect relevant information. A statement of services, often provided by a former employer, will focus only on the most advanced levels of professional accomplishments. The researchers, however, raised several issues about the standard process for collecting candidate information. In particular, they mentioned how time-consuming it is to acquire information since it might take days to locate a credible source offering relevant data on the applicant. The time gets wasted when previous employers are unreachable or preoccupied with their work during the research phase or in case the business shuts down. It must be well worked upon when it would be most beneficial to collect data, such as when employees in various time zones are at home (Spence, 2018).

Furthermore, recruiters are still vulnerable to getting fabricated data since the most prevalent source of applicant information is the individual's most recent employer. Most hiring managers will contact the most recent employer to prevent wasting time. In some instances, hiring someone before learning their whole past might be dangerous since the job history records of candidates may not be available. Since the employee's most recent statement of service probably only featured good remarks, they have no reference to draw on in times of disagreement or aberrant workplace behaviour. Getting relevant information might be difficult when a candidate's former employer is no longer in business. By assisting a business in taking appropriate measures to lessen the possibility of errors, the blockchain network may bring about several positive outcomes. For instance, after an employee's work history has been authenticated, the network stores it so that future employers do not have to look for it themselves; this is made possible by the network's complicated but straightforward style of functioning. A candidate's employment history may be compiled into a single document serving as an employment record, eliminating the need for a statement of service. The network has nothing but positive results on businesses since it streamlines the onerous process of information collection by eliminating the need for third-party verification of job history and making that information readily available to all users. Therefore, a person will have a secure online repository for their complete and comprehensive career history, which can be accessed by both the individual and any prospective or existing employers. The blockchain system also ensures that workers' employment records are preserved during a business's demise, an essential safeguard for sensitive data. Guest (2022) states that it gives companies the most accurate overview of a candidate's qualifications and history. Because of their limited means, SMBs and their individual owners stand to gain the most from this innovative technology. In addition, many organizations in this sector often underinvest in employee and owner professional development through inadequate funding for training programmes. Further, individuals often need more resources and time while regularly attending professional programmes (Walker, 2017).

Finally, the organization's current and future talent requirements are often disregarded for more urgent tasks. Blockchain technology is helpful in these situations because a database can be used to find qualified candidates for open positions based on specific criteria, and it can also provide training and education opportunities for existing staff members. In addition, the database might provide essential details about the organization's requirements and the special education or experience workers or applicants need to possess to meet them. Because this is handled automatically by the system utilizing existing data, the HR department no longer has to deal with it, which benefits their time and productivity. Applicants may learn more about the company than is on their résumé, and any remarks regarding praise or criticism discovered in their ledger cannot be changed or withdrawn, as indicated by Aishwarya (2018). It facilitates the hiring process by highlighting individuals with superior qualifications and experience. Blockchain technology may help prevent "Resume Polishers" from misleading perspective employers with embellished or entirely fabricated credentials. Education verification, media and civil records, credit reports on employers, criminal histories, sex offender records, and driver's licenses are all examples of applicant information that recruiters may access using blockchain. As a final benefit, blockchain technology may standardize career profiles, increasing the quality of CV material and records and monitoring an employee's professional growth over time (Yaga and Mell, 2018).

8.8 Evidence of Blockchain in Global Markets

In this chapter, we have looked at how new technologies, particularly blockchain, are reshaping HR functions in companies and posing new issues and opportunities. Companies in today's highly competitive global market are being pushed to the brink by the need to keep up with the competition. There is growing evidence that blockchain is being used in HR, and more significantly in the hiring process, to significant effect on businesses. While just around 0.5% of companies worldwide were utilizing blockchain technology in 2019, the demand for it is rising quickly, and it is predicted that 80% of companies will be using some blockchain concept within the next decade. Blockchain's purported capacity to revolutionize company procedures influences HR practices and is said to increase openness, precision, and trust in HR administration. It emphasizes that the technical performance of emerging technologies, and blockchain, will help "overall systemic risk reduction" and operational enhancements. Businesses must investigate blockchain's capabilities and the feasibility of using this emerging technology in their HR procedures (Yi, Yung, Fong, and Tripathi, 2020).

The widespread use of blockchain in the HR sector can improve working conditions for everyone involved. Since HR departments discover other uses for the technology, it will become easier and faster to check and hire new employees. It will increase blockchain's value as it will help find the appropriate person for the job with less hassle. One of the primary areas of interest for new technology researchers, which this article has proposed, is the efficiency and advantages of employing blockchain searching in the recruiting process.

Using a system that will give safety while confirming the transaction source is essential for rampant fraud, hacking, and ransomware. In addition, HR departments now must deal with a broader set of challenges than ever before. Identifying, screening, and reviewing applicants, as well as completing validation checks and authenticating documents, takes much time, but avoiding the danger of inadequate hiring is necessary. Companies spend significant money on external firms to help them find and hire qualified employees and rely on them to negotiate favourable contract terms. In addition, businesses spend much cash on hiring and training new workers to learn that the new hire is not a good fit and start the process all over again. The incorrect person is hired, which may have disastrous effects on an organization's morale, production, and finances. Since data is maintained in a virtual immutable ledger, preventing recruiting issues may have substantial benefits for HR departments that, in turn, help the whole organization by making it easier for recruiters to check a candidate's profile online reliably and efficiently.

8.9 Conclusion

In conclusion, blockchain has the potential to provide considerable benefits in the form of enhanced productivity, heightened security, enhanced traceability, and increased transparency. Blockchain's many applications are rapidly expanding, and it is up to the HR experts involved to weigh their importance and find ways to use them so their companies may gain a competitive edge. Blockchain will profoundly impact HRM as it becomes more popular and publicly available, and blockchain will eventually become an essential HR tool utilized by all successful companies.

References

Aishwarya, N. (2018). Potential Impact of Blockchain on HR and People Management. *International Journal of Emerging Technologies and Innovative Research*, 5(9), 127–129. http://www.jetir.org/view?paper=JETIRA006284

Berwal, P., Dhatterwal, J.S., Kaswan, K.S. and Kant, S. (2022). *Computer Applications in Engineering and Management*. CRC Press.

Dhatterwal, J.S., Kaswan, K.S., Jaglan, V. and Vij, A. (2022a). Machine Learning and Deep Learning Algorithms for IoD. In *The Internet of Drones* (pp. 237–292). Apple Academic Press.

Dhatterwal, J.S., Kaswan, K.S. and Ojha, R.P. (2022b). The Role of Multiagent System in Industry 4.0. In *A Roadmap for Enabling Industry 4.0 by Artificial Intelligence* (pp. 227–246). Wiley.

Elayan, M.B. (2021). *Transformation of Human Resources Management Solutions as a Strategic Tool for GIG Workers Contracting*. Institute of Public Administration.

Fachrunnisa, O. and Hussain, F. (2020). Blockchain-Based Human Resource Management Practices for Mitigating Skills and Competencies Gap in Workforce. *International Journal of Engineering Business Management*, 12, 3.

Fremont, V. and Jonathan, G. (2018). Can Blockchain Technology Solve Trust Issues in Industrial Networks? In: *17th International Conference Perspectives in Business Informatics Research*. BIR Workshops, p. 401.

Guest, D (2022). How blockchain can innovate recruiting process (https://www.dice.com/career-advice/how-blockchain-could-innovate-the-recruiting-process)

Kaswan, K.S., Dhatterwal, J.S. and Kumar, K. (2021). Blockchain of Internet of Things-Based Earthquake Alarming System in Smart Cities. In *Integration and Implementation of the Internet of Things Through Cloud Computing* (pp. 272–287). IGI Global.

Kaswan, K.S., Dhatterwal, J.S., Kumar, S. and Lal, S. (2022). Cybersecurity Law-Based Insurance Market. In *Big Data: A Game Changer for Insurance Industry* (pp. 303–321). Emerald Publishing Limited.

Kaswan, K.S., Dhatterwal, J.S., Sood, K. and Balusamy, B. (2022). Role of Blockchain Technology in the Modern Era. In *Blockchain Technology in Corporate Governance: Transforming Business and Industries* (pp. 1–28). Wiley.

Lukić, J., Salkić, H. and Ostojić, B. (2018). New job positions and recruitment of employees shaped by blockchain technologies. *Fourth International Scientific Business Conference LIMEN 2018-Leadership & Management: Integrated Politics of Research and Innovations*. pp. 314–320. https://www.researchgate.net/publication/330959205_NEW_JOB_POSITIONS_AND_RECRUITMENT_OF_EMPLOYEES_SHAPED_BY_BLOCKCHAIN_TECHNOLOGIES

Makridakis, S. and Christodoulou, K. (2019). Blockchain: Current Challenges and Future Prospects/Applications. *Future Internet*, 11, 1–16. https://www.mdpi.com/1999-5903/11/12/258

Nascimento, S., Pólvora A., Anderberg A., Andonova E., Bellia M., Calès L., Inamorato dos Santos A., Kounelis I., Nai Fovino I., Petracco Giudici M., Papanagiotou E., Sobolewski M., Rossetti F., Spirito L. (2019). Blockchain Now

And Tomorrow: Assessing Multidimensional Impacts of Distributed Ledger Technologies, (pp 17–19). EUR 29813 EN, Publications Office of the European Union, Luxembourg, doi:10.2760/901029, JRC117255

Neiheiser, R. Inácio, G., et al. (2019). HRM Smart Contracts on the Blockchain. In: 2019 IEEE Symposium on Computers and Communications (ISCC). IEEE.

Onik, M., Miraz, M. and Kim, C. (2018). A Recruitment and Human Resource Management Technique Using Blockchain Technology for Industry 4.0. Smart Cities Symposium, p. 1.

Pinna, A. and Ibba, S. (2017). A Blockchain-Based Decentralized System for Proper Handling of Temporary Employment Contracts. *Advances in Intelligent Systems and Computing, 2,* DOI: 10.1007/978-3-030-01177-2_88.

Salleh, F. Radzi, R., et al. (2019). New Information Management Dimension in Blockchain. *International Journal of Academic Research in Business and Social Sciences*, 8(12), 1384–1385.

Samani, H., et al. (2012). Towards Robotics Leadership: An Analysis of Leadership Characteristics and the Roles Robots Will Inherit in Future Human Society. *Asian Conference on Intelligent Information and Database Systems* (pp. 158–165). Springer.

Sarda, P. Chowdhury, M., et al. (2018). Blockchain for Fraud Prevention: A Work-History Fraud Prevention System. In: *17th IEEE International Conference on Trust, Security and Privacy in Computing and Communications and 12th IEEE International Conference on Big Data Science and Engineering. Institute of Electrical and Electronics Engineers*, pp. 1–3.

Sauppé, A. and Mutlu, B. (2015). The social impact of a robot co-worker in industrial settings. Proceedings of the 33rd Annual ACM Conference on Human Factors in Computing Systems.

Spence, A. (2018). *Blockchain and the Chief Human Resources Officer. Transforming the HR Function and the Market for Skills, Talent, and Training.* Brightline Initiative and the Blockchain Research Institute.

Walker, D. (2017). The Hidden Risks of Recruitment: How to Recognize Them and Protect Your Organization. CV Check, pp. 4–9.

Yaga, D. Mell, P., et al. (2018). Blockchain Technology Overview (pp. 1–15). NIST. https://www.nist.gov/publications/blockchain-technology-overview (Accessed 19 February 2021).

Yi, C., Yung, E., Fong, C. and Tripathi, S. (2020). Benefits and Use of Blockchain Technology to Human Resources Management: A Critical Review. *International Journal of Human Resource Studies*, 10(2), 13.

Chapter 9

A Study on Value Creation in HR Using Blockchain Technology

Bikrant Kesari

Maulana Azad National Institute of Technology, Bhopal, India

9.1 Introduction

The use of blockchain technology in human resources (HR) is becoming more popular, and we are here to discuss the reasons for this trend. Blockchain technology is rapidly spreading across many sectors, including the HR sector (Chillakuri & Attili, 2021). Information is essential to business. It is best if it is received quickly and accurately. Blockchain is the best technology for delivering such information. It offers instant, shareable, and fully transparent data that is recorded on a blockchain network and accessed only by members of a permitted network. Blockchains are shared databases or ledgers among computer network nodes that store data digitally. This database is copied and shared among a group of computers that form a network. Network members can update the data or records kept in the ledger. It functions independently of any need for a centralized authority to be present. The information stored on blockchain is organized into immutable blocks that are interconnected. Decentralization and cryptographic hashing are used in blockchain technology, which helps make the history of any digital data visible and unalterable (Zheng et al., 2017). Blockchains are digital ledgers containing cryptographically signed

DOI: 10.4324/9781003372622-9

transactions that are distributed and organized into blocks. After validation and a consensus decision, each block is cryptographically associated with the preceding block.

When new blocks are introduced, it becomes increasingly more work to change existing ones (creating tamper resistance). Therefore, new blocks are duplicated across all copies of the ledger inside the network, and any disputes are automatically handled using predetermined criteria (Yaga et al., 2018).

9.2 History of Blockchain Technology

Stuart Haber and W. Scott Stornetta created blockchain technology in 1991. The researchers provide a computationally viable method for securely time-stamping digital documents that cannot be altered or retroactively updated. They made an approach based on a chain block that will be accessed only after going through a cryptographically secure process to keep the time-stamped papers safe. Merkle Trees were added to the blockchain in 1992, making it more efficient by combining several documents into one block. Merkle Trees provide a "secured chain of blocks." Each data record was linked to the previous one. The last document in this chain includes the chain's history. However, this invention was never implemented, and the patent expired in 2004. In 2008, Satoshi Nakamoto proposed distributed blockchains. By improving the design, he adds blocks to the original chain without the responsible parties' signatures (Nakamoto, 2008). The redesigned trees would store data exchanges securely. Each trade is dated and validated using a peer-to-peer network governed without a central authority. These advancements provided the basis for blockchain-based cryptocurrencies.

According to Global Blockchain Survey Report 2020 by Deloitte, about 40% of respondents integrated blockchain into production, and the other 55% envisioned it as their upcoming strategic plan (Global Blockchain Survey, 2019). There is a growing interest in combining blockchain technology with artificial intelligence (AI) to improve business operations (Pandey & Khaskel, 2019). An intersection of blockchain, AR/VR, and web3 gave rise to Metaverse. Several start-ups inspired by COVID-19 pandemic work-from-home culture started working on virtual world creation. However, various alternative applications for blockchain technology are being researched, evaluated, and developed, such as smart contracts for software-defined networks in the supply chain and several other industries, including entertainment, healthcare, transportation, and real estate.

9.3 Blockchain-Based Value Creation in HR

In recent years, great attention has been paid to using blockchain technology in HR, especially in the Internet age, as it could improve the effectiveness and productivity of applications in business ecosystems. Value is the amount of the sum of all current and future values generated by all players in the value system, where value production means increasing the total value created by all participants (Abdollahi et al., 2022). The most potential uses of blockchain technology are those that solve significant problems in human resource management (HRM), such as compensation, recruiting, employee verification, and contract administration (Ramachandran et al., 2022) (Figure 9.1). The organization needs to have creative workers to ensure future development and success (Kabalina & Osipova, 2022). There will be a positive relationship between factors related to technological readiness and organizational career development, such as getting closer to

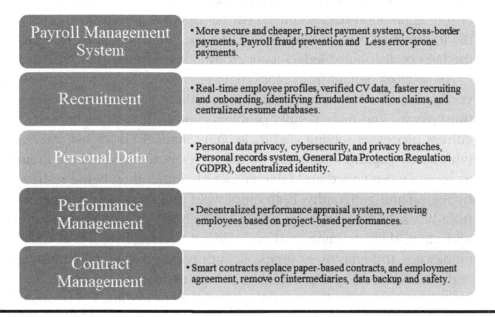

Figure 9.1 Blockchain in HR. (Cunha et al., 2021; Ghadge et al., 2022; Li et al., 2021; Jani et al., 2021; Salah et al., 2020; Sharif & Ghodoosi, 2022; Shi et al., 2021; Sifah et al., 2020; Tan & Sundarakani, 2020, Review of Existing Literature.)

goals, getting better at skills, getting promoted more quickly, and getting paid more (Dhankhar & Singh, 2022).

i. ***Blockchain in Payroll*** – Blockchain has the potential to simplify and speed up many aspects of global payroll and international payments. Blockchain allows for considerably faster cross-border payments than the present BACS or wire transfer systems, even those requiring currency exchanges. In addition, by eliminating intermediaries like banks and clearinghouses and enabling the application of currency rates in real-time, payments may be confirmed via the distributed ledger, always ensuring maximum accuracy (Tyma et al., 2022). Blockchain application also paves the way for investigating other approaches to employee compensation (Chillakuri & Attili, 2021). To begin, this may include providing workers with digital wallets to get paid quickly and perhaps subsequently use the money compared to how they would use Apple Pay or Google Pay. In addition, it would provide flexibility in how companies send payments to an international workforce and autonomy in how workers access and use their earnings.

ii. ***Blockchain in the recruitment process*** – HR managers want accurate and validated applicant data to prevent fraudulent resumes and applications from entering the system and, worse, from getting picked. To ensure application data accuracy, HR managers may retrieve and validate the information using a blockchain database, which could be done with the help of distributed ledger technology (Rhemananda et al., 2020).

HR services benefit from blockchain technology, such as trustworthy verification of counterparties' identities without the participation of a third party – and then identify problems and inefficiencies in their current processes solving via blockchain (Sharif & Ghodoosi, 2022), which may expand a company's pool of applicants and enable them to source more varied and talented people rather than being restricted by region and geography. Both employees and employers will benefit from blockchain technology, which not only keeps a reliable record of education, skills, training, and professional performance but also lets employees and employers access it. Supplying prospective employers with this "value id," people might leverage their talents, training, and experience into actual value in the employment market. Using analytics in business data can better match people to positions (Jani et al., 2021). Thus, blockchain is most effective when used to automate and stream-line HRM recruitment processes, which in turn saves time, increases accuracy, and helps HRM workers become more productive.

iii. ***Personal data and privacy protection*** – Data breaches have exposed millions of names, emails, passwords, addresses, birth dates, and financial information due to unauthorized access to an organization's database. It enables cybercriminals to access passwords, credit card details, social security numbers, and financial information. Blockchain and AI may protect personal information. Users have a choice over what, when, and how much of their personal information may be exchanged and with whom via decentralized and federated identity systems. These solutions also help mitigate cybersecurity risks. AI improves blockchain-based privacy solutions by giving clients more control over their data and ensuring that the data and its models are more accurate, fair, and reliable (Heister & Yuthas, 2022). The General Data Protection Regulation (GDPR), which the European Union enacted in 2016, is the benchmark for privacy laws across the globe regarding protecting personal data security. Protecting personal information and property is made easy using zero-knowledge proofs. In zero-knowledge proofs, the "prover" may convince the "verifier" that something about them is true without disclosing personal information.

iv. ***Blockchain in performance management*** – HR managers may verify the authenticity of data like employee hours worked and completed assignments using blockchain technology. Moreover, by connecting the wages, salaries, and bonuses to it, HR managers can make timely payments to the workers without going through each of their records. In addition to being an essential record-keeping task, performance management should complete as a private ledger. Each year, a block will establish that comprises that year's goal-setting, agreed-upon objectives, and all necessary measures (Salah et al., 2020). This section is accessible to all organization members to add comments, praise, or areas for improvement. When an assignment is issued, the associated manager may include a block that the line manager can verify and skip-level manager of both assignees and assign in conjunction with HR, if required (Kuruppu et al., 2022). After completing the assignment, the assignee will offer comments for that block. If an error occurs, the validation procedure will indicate the error. Transparency within the process and the elimination of subjectivity or prejudice will undoubtedly improve the employee experience (Fachrunnisa & Hussain, 2020). Furthermore, final comments are stored on the identical blockchain and confirmed.

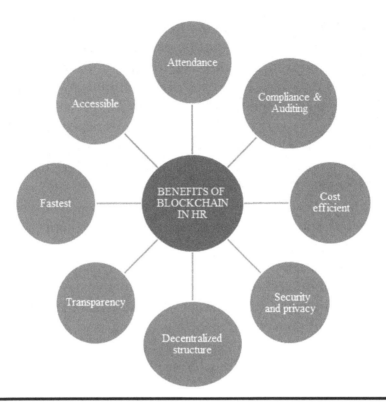

Figure 9.2   Benefits of blockchain in HR. (Authors Representation.)

  v. ***Contract management solutions and Blockchain*** – Contract
     management is software with all the tools and methods needed
     to handle the contract lifecycle. It takes care of the contracts from
     customers, employees, partners, and other entities that depend on
     contracts to keep their work going. In contract management, blockchain
     is a digital ledger that is both decentralized and transparent, designed
     to record almost any transaction (Mathivathanan et al., 2021). Every
     stage of the contracting process results in notifications, alerts, and the
     creation of a shared ledger of all activity for all parties involved (Tan &
     Sundarakani, 2020). Consequently, clear-cut contracts with versions and
     activity history can be tracked and saved electronically in a single area
     and are only accessible by the parties having access (Figure 9.2).

9.4 Value of Blockchain Technology in Human Resources Management

Implementing blockchain technology can potentially transform the current
HRs significantly practises by introducing novel and effective enhancements.

Blockchain technology aligns intending to optimize and expedite each process within the HRM value chain.

i. ***Attendance*** – Blockchain technology stores fingerprints and iris scans for legal ID and record-keeping. Close watch on employee data such as payroll and reimbursement expenses. The real-time data would be accessible to HR, confirming the records' accuracy. It makes it easier to trust the payment authorization process and examine claims. In addition, this would make it easier for the HR and payroll departments to work together and make fewer mistakes.

ii. ***Compliance and auditing*** – Implementing blockchain technology for compliance and auditing purposes is easy to conduct as the data stored in the blockchain are already accurate and validated. Moreover, it connects all people, activities, and communications that assign in-house talent and third-party suppliers, cross-functional communications, and the activities they were assigned to do or tie in performance-based. As a result, HR can comply with increasingly stringent regulations (Kuruppu et al., 2022).

iii. ***Cost-efficient*** – Using blockchain, HR departments may significantly reduce expenses related to third-party providers. Blockchain has no inherited centralized participant, so there are no vendor fees to pay. In addition, less engagement is required to authenticate a transaction, eliminating the need to invest money or time in HR operations (Cunha et al., 2021).

iv. ***Security and privacy*** – Regarding transaction security, blockchain is not just the cutting-edge technology of today but also the leading technology. Applications built on blockchain technology give users more confidence in protecting their data storage, given that they can only customize their information to their own goals. The primary objectives of blockchain-based applications are to improve user authentication and restrict access to critical infrastructure (Koh et al., 2020).

v. ***Decentralized database*** – The distributed database of information is the foundation of blockchain technology. By leveraging this technology, information shared through a decentralized database is highly resistant to unauthorized modifications (Yaga et al., 2018). Information is stored in numerous host computers, allowing a community of users to access shared information safely. In addition, the decentralized nature of blockchain protects user data and ensures that invalid information is not permitted to add the chain (Sifah et al., 2020).

vi. ***Transparency*** – HR departments have established more laws and regulations to increase openness (Tyma et al., 2022). However, with the aid of blockchain, the company may choose a decentralized network without a central authority, enhancing the system's transparency (Mathivathanan et al., 2021).

vii. ***Fastest*** – Blockchain technology has improved the efficiency of employee workflows in minutes rather than days or weeks, quicker and speedier decision-making in recruitment, onboarding (Ghadge et al., 2022), learning and development, payrolls, and talent acquisition. Blockchain technology allows instant access to information, speeding up the process, and giving them more accuracy in less time.

viii. ***Accessible*** – Blockchain technology can easily access the daily work of everyone in the HR department, from recruiters to top executives. It encompasses various aspects of HRM such as recruitment, talent acquisition, background verification, job history validation, smart contract-based engagement of contract workers, onboarding, employee data management, financial transactions, and employee administration.

9.5 Key Findings

Blockchain disruption has been the most discussed in payments and financial markets. Regarding HR, blockchain can help the recruitment process with background checks and verifying applicants' credentials so that they may be placed in the most suitable positions and workers while safeguarding all sensitive information relating to them and the organization itself. Blockchain-based smart contracts facilitate tracking job completion and the automatic release of funds. As a result, transactions between firms can be more quickly, reliably, and safely. Smart contracts between a company and its employees give both parties a clear idea of the terms, the ability to turn a contract on and off as needed and provide benefits at the right time. From a payroll and HR viewpoint, it is evident that blockchain can revolutionize the industry. In a corporate environment that is becoming more international, saving the cost and time of the HR department has a significant positive effect and promotes the improved experiences that the organization wants. It is time to start investigating these prospects and improving payroll and HR to benefit workers and companies. Further, individuals who provide personal information greatly benefit from using zero-knowledge proofs to protect their privacy and exercise control over their property rights. With the use of blockchain technology, performance management systems may be redesigned with decentralized governing bodies (Distributed Ledger System).

9.6 Managerial Implication

The Blockchain is a unique device that allows safe transactions without a central authority. It has been studied for implementation in numerous domains and functions, but HRM has garnered far more attention than other functional areas (Javaid et al., 2021). Therefore, this chapter contributes significantly to understanding blockchain adoption in HRM practices. This report provides HR professionals involved in blockchain projects with valuable insights into emerging HR process areas. In addition, blockchain has many potential uses in HRM processes that were previously indecisive, such as database creation, employing new staff, tax policy, the replacement of work contracts with smart contracts, payroll, HR accounting, and performance evaluation (Ramachandran et al., 2022).

9.7 Conclusion

Data may be shared and combined in ways never before possible because of the fast development of blockchain technologies. HR processes have benefited from these technological advancements in the context of digital transformation. Blockchain technology offers safe and private data exchange while providing individuals complete power over their information by introducing unique mechanisms like decentralized identities and zero-knowledge proofs. These innovations may lead to more secure systems and more ethical handling of personal data. Participants in a blockchain may accomplish these goals by developing efficient governance structures and procedures. HR practitioners must prioritize transparency and trust in company processes while managing human capital in a competitive climate (Koh et al., 2020; Ruhela & Pandey, 2022). Blockchain technology has numerous potential uses, including disrupting employment, payroll, taxes, benefit administration, data storage etc. However, the technical performance of blockchain technology, such as its encryption and pinpoint precision, is unquestionably impressive. The success of blockchain will depend on how well it can make an organization's processes more trustworthy and open.

Blockchain is a phenomenal, unpredictable power. It is already wreaking havoc on several firms. Businesses adopting blockchain technology are now securing their place in an ever-changing environment (Abdollahi et al., 2022). Firms will face an immense challenge if they do not invest in this technology.

References

Abdollahi, A., Sadeghvaziri, F., & Rejeb, A. (2022, March 25). Exploring the role of blockchain technology in value creation: a multiple case study approach. Quality & Quantity, 57(1), 427–451. https://doi.org/10.1007/s11135-022-01348-2

Chillakuri, B., & Attili, V. S. P. (2021, March 22). Role of blockchain in HR's response to new-normal. International Journal of Organizational Analysis, 30(6), 1359–1378. https://doi.org/10.1108/ijoa-08-2020-2363

Cunha, P. R. D., Soja, P., & Themistocleous, M. (2021, June 21). Blockchain for development: a guiding framework. Information Technology for Development, 27(3), 417–438. https://doi.org/10.1080/02681102.2021.1935453

Dhankhar, K., & Singh, A. (2022, October 7). Employees' adoption of HR analytics – a theoretical framework based on career construction theory. Evidence-Based HRM: A Global Forum for Empirical Scholarship. https://doi.org/10.1108/ebhrm-02-2022-0053

Fachrunnisa, O., & Hussain, F. K. (2020, January 1). Blockchain-based human resource management practices for mitigating skills and competencies gap in the workforce. International Journal of Engineering Business Management, 12, 184797902096640. https://doi.org/10.1177/1847979020966400

Ghadge, A., Bourlakis, M., Kimble, S., & Seuring, S. (2022, October 5). Blockchain implementation in pharmaceutical supply chains: a review and conceptual framework. International Journal of Production Research, 1–19. https://doi.org/10.1080/00207543.2022.2125595

Global Blockchain survey. (2019, May 10). Deloitte Ireland. https://www2.deloitte.com/ie/en/pages/technology/articles/Global_Blockchain_survey.html (Accessed February 8, 2023).

Heister, S., & Yuthas, K. (2022, January 12). How blockchain and AI enable personal data privacy and support cybersecurity. Blockchain Potential in AI. https://doi.org/10.5772/intechopen.96999

Jani, A., Muduli, A., & Kishore, K. (2021, October 7). Human resource transformation in India: examining the role digital human resource technology and human resource role. International Journal of Organizational Analysis. https://doi.org/10.1108/ijoa-08-2021-2886

Javaid, M., Haleem, A., Pratap Singh, R., Khan, S., & Suman, R. (2021, December). Blockchain technology applications for Industry 4.0: a literature-based review. Blockchain: Research and Applications, 2(4), 100027. https://doi.org/10.1016/j.bcra.2021.100027

Kabalina, V., & Osipova, A. (2022, April 22). Identifying and assessing talent potential for the future needs of a company. Journal of Management Development, 41(3), 147–162. https://doi.org/10.1108/jmd-11-2021-0319

Koh, L., Dolgui, A., & Sarkis, J. (2020, April 2). Blockchain in transport and logistics – paradigms and transitions. International Journal of Production Research, 58(7), 2054–2062. https://doi.org/10.1080/00207543.2020.1736428

Kuruppu, S. C., Dissanayake, D., & de Villiers, C. (2022, February 24). How can NGO accountability practices be improved with technologies such as blockchain and triple-entry accounting? Accounting, Auditing & Accountability Journal, 35(7), 1714–1742. https://doi.org/10.1108/aaaj-10-2020-4972

Li, K., Lee, J. Y., & Gharehgozli, A. (2021, September 13). Blockchain in food supply chains: a literature review and synthesis analysis of platforms, benefits and challenges. International Journal of Production Research, 1–20. https://doi.org/10.1080/00207543.2021.1970849

Mathivathanan, D., Mathiyazhagan, K., Rana, N. P., Khorana, S., & Dwivedi, Y. K. (2021, January 12). Barriers to the adoption of blockchain technology in business supply chains: a total interpretive structural modelling (TISM) approach. International Journal of Production Research, 59(11), 3338–3359. https://doi.org/10.1080/00207543.2020.1868597

Nakamoto, S. (2008). "Bitcoin: a peer-to-peer electronic cash system," available at: https://bitcoin.org/bitcoin.pdf (Accessed February 8, 2023).

Pandey, S., & Khaskel, P. (2019). Application of AI in human resource management and Gen Y's reaction. International Journal of Recent Technology and Engineering (IJRTE), 8(4), 10325–10331.

Ramachandran, R., Babu, V., & Murugesan, V. P. (2022, November 29). The role of blockchain technology in the process of decision-making in human resource management: a review and future research agenda. Business Process Management Journal, 29(1), 116–139. https://doi.org/10.1108/bpmj-07-2022-0351

Rhemananda, H., Simbolon, D. R., & Fachrunnisa, O. (2020, November 28). Blockchain Technology to Support Employee Recruitment and Selection in Industrial Revolution 4.0. Proceedings of International Conference on Smart Computing and Cyber Security, 305–311. https://doi.org/10.1007/978-981-15-7990-5_30

Ruhela, V., & Pandey, S. (2022). Emotional intelligence, conflict management styles and innovative work behaviour - a study on Indian employees. International Journal of Early Childhood Special Education, 14(4), 2678–2684.

Salah, D., Ahmed, M. H., & ElDahshan, K. (2020, April 15). Blockchain Applications in Human Resources Management. Proceedings of the Evaluation and Assessment in Software Engineering. https://doi.org/10.1145/3383219.3383274

Sharif, M. M., & Ghodoosi, F. (2022, February 2). The ethics of blockchain in organizations. Journal of Business Ethics, 178(4), 1009–1025. https://doi.org/10.1007/s10551-022-05058-5

Shi, X., Yao, S., & Luo, S. (2021, August 31). Innovative platform operations with the use of technologies in the blockchain era. International Journal of Production Research, 1–19. https://doi.org/10.1080/00207543.2021.1953182

Sifah, E. B., Xia, H., Cobblah, C. N. A., Xia, Q., Gao, J., & Du, X. (2020). BEMPAS: a decentralized employee performance assessment system based on blockchain for smart City governance. IEEE Access, p. 8, 99528–99539. https://doi. org/10.1109/access.2020.2997650

Tan, W. K. A., & Sundarakani, B. (2020, September 22). Assessing blockchain technology application for freight booking business: a case study from technology acceptance model perspective. Journal of Global Operations and Strategic Sourcing, 14(1), 202–223. https://doi.org/10.1108/jgoss-04-2020-0018

Tyma, B., Dhillon, R., Sivabalan, P., & Wieder, B. (2022, February 4). Understanding accountability in blockchain systems. Accounting, Auditing & Accountability Journal, 35(7), 1625–1655. https://doi.org/10.1108/aaaj-07-2020-4713

Yaga, D., Mell, P., Roby, N., & Scarfone, K. (2018, October). Blockchain technology overview. https://doi.org/10.6028/nist.ir.8202

Zheng, Z., Xie, S., Dai, H., Chen, X., & Wang, H. (2017, June). An Overview of Blockchain Technology: Architecture, Consensus, and Future Trends. 2017 IEEE International Congress on Big Data (BigData Congress). https://doi. org/10.1109/bigdatacongress.2017.85

Chapter 10

Organizational Factors Affecting Innovative HR Practices and Systems: A Way to Creating the New Gen Workplace

Suhasini Choudhury, Mahuya Ghosh Dutta, and Padmalita Routray
Fakir Mohan University, Balasore, India

Ashok Kumar Dash
Ravenshaw University, Cuttack, India

10.1 Introduction

Around 2.56 billion (30% of the global population) of people worldwide belong to Generation Z (born in 1997–2012). They are also forecasted to be 27% of the workforce by 2025 (Staglin, 2022). This is clear that in the near future, this new generation will handle the responsibility of economic growth and sustainability. So, it becomes essential to analyze their characteristics and behavior. Though they share some similarities with millennials (born in 1981–1996), they differ significantly in their behavior and characteristics. This generation started becoming operative during the economic recession with a high unemployment rate and rapid growth of

DOI: 10.4324/9781003372622-10

the Internet and mobile services (Turner, 2015; Ngoc Thang et al., 2022). So, they have completely different cultural values and practices, which the managers need to understand to create a perfect working environment for the employees of a new generation. Therefore, understanding Generation Z behavior is essential for leaders and managers. Accordingly, it is necessary to design effective human resources (HR) practices and systems to give this new generation of employees a realistic job preview and workplace coaching and to foster communication effectiveness for handling diversity, equity, and inclusion in the workplace. Their study shows flexible work practices, recognition and rewards, pay and perks, volunteering and seeking feedback in organizations; Generation Z. Aggarwal et al. (2022) found that effective task performance achieved by implementing innovative HR practices leads to satisfaction and practical organizational commitment. Due to competitive constraints, firms have proactively identified HR issues and implemented more creative HR strategies (Khatri & Budhwar, 2002; Agarwala, 2003).

The new generation expects high cooperation from the top managers and their peers, especially in knowledge sharing and transfer (Bencsik et al., 2016). They have a high-value proposition, unlike the millennials who desire the vertical growth of their rank. They prefer informal and digital communication through text, emojis, and video calls. Continuous feedback is the need of them (Turner, 2015). They expect their leader should be friendly, open-minded, fair and confident leadership and should posit a positive attitude (Grow & Yang, 2018). They also seek internal growth opportunities and development in the workplace (Adecco, 2016). To meet these expectations for effective performance, business leaders or employers are suggested to focus on the points viz. prioritizing and implementing mental health at work, introducing them to a hybrid way of working and flexibility, recognizing and preventing burnout, the epithetical approach of leaders, long-term well-being of workforce (Global Talent, 2022). Considering the stress pattern and anxieties in this generation, they should be taken care of their mental health and wellness in organizations. To deal with these factors, managers should act as a coach to reduce their anxieties and provide them with a sense of autonomy for a project to reduce stress (Schroth, 2019). Soft skills or life skills training is justified to be incorporated.

The most critical resource is the planned and thorough approach to managing an organization's employees, called human resource management (HRM) (Ramkumar & Rajini, 2018). For years, the research on the role of HR practices in shaping human capital's attitude and behavior in achieving organizational performance has caught the attention of scholars, practitioners, business leaders, and managers (Gardner et al., 2001; Kehoe & Wright, 2013; Chaudhary, 2020). In today's era, the role of HR practices in developing and boosting human resources to gain a competitive advantage is vital (Collins & Clark, 2003). The HRM must move from traditional HR practices to the new set of HR practices as per the need of the current requirement (Agarwala, 2003). Innovations in HR practices are vital for an organization's goal achievement in changing context (Agarwala, 2003). HR managers are getting ready to shape the behavior and attitude of the new generation by using the experiences of millennials and Generation X (Schroth, 2019).

Many studies have been done on innovation factors (Branzei & Vertinsky, 2006; Mol & Birkinshaw, 2009; Ganter & Hecker, 2013; Kawasaki, 2015) or innovation practices (Al-Ansari, 2014; Zeraatkar et al., 2020). Research has also been undertaken on the relationship between HR practices and Generation Z individually and collectively (Arar & Öneren, 2018; Chillakuri, 2020; Barhate & Dirani, 2022). Very negligible studies have been incorporated on the organizational factors affecting innovative HR practices and how innovative HR practices play a crucial role in creating a compatible workplace fit for Gen Zers. The COVID-19 pandemic has brought attention to the world's mental health issues, and debates about it are becoming more prevalent in all spheres of society, including the workplace. The survey reveals that Gen Zs and millennials have appreciated their employers' efforts, with the majority of the respondents (57% of Gen Z and 53% of millennials) agreeing that workplace well-being and mental well-being have become more of a priority for their employers since the onset of the pandemic. Most of the respondents, 53% of Gen X and 51% of millennials, felt that while their organization now speaks more about mental well-being, this has not significantly influenced employees. Unfortunately, for many respondents, this has not yet transformed into meaningful positive change (Global Talent, 2022). So, the objectives of the study are threefold as mentioned here:

1. To identify the characteristics and expectations of Generation Z from the workplace
2. To explore the organizational factors affecting innovative HR practices
3. To explore the role of innovative HR practices in creating a workplace suitable for Generation Z

10.2 Methodology

The study adopted the systematic literature review on organizational factors affecting innovative HR practices suitable for a new-generation (Gen Z) workplace (Refer Table 10.1). We considered both quantitative and qualitative papers for our review.

10.2.1 The Time Horizon for the Selection of Papers

We considered articles till December 2022 to explore all the documents related to this topic. We did not restrict time for searching articles as only a little study has been done on the related field. We found relevant articles from 2001.

10.2.2 Selection of Databases

The research has used the Scopus database to explore the studies related to organizational factors, HR practices, and new-generation workplaces because the Scopus database is considered a good source for management and social science subject area (Palomo et al., 2017). Apart from this, we searched Google Scholar to identify the related papers. We also considered some survey reports published very recently to identify the problem. The research considered the articles published in the English language and business management, accounting and finance and social science subject areas.

10.2.3 Searching and Selecting Articles

An initial search on the electronic database using the keywords; factors affecting process innovation, organizational factors and innovation, HR practices, new generation or Generation Z, innovative HR practices, and new-generation workplace yielded 109,795 articles. After selecting documents on social science and business management, finance and accounting, we reduced to 3,938 documents. Based on observation (looking at article titles), 567 were related. By screening the abstract of each article, 189 articles were shortlisted. The excluded articles were not relevant to our context. Finally, 39 articles were considered for review after going through the entire paper. Figure 10.1 displays a PRISMA diagram developed by Moher et al. (2009) to show the information flow across the four stages of the systematic review. (Source: Information flows across the various review steps taken from Moher et al. (2009)).

Table 10.1   Contribution of Authors of Studies Organizational Factors Impacting Innovative HR Practices in Creating New-Generation Workplaces

Organizational factor	Innovative HR practices	New-generation workplace
Firm size (Damanpour & Gopalakrishnan, 2001; Branzei & Vertinsky, 2006; Damanpour & Schneider, 2006; Mol & Birkinshaw, 2009; Naranjo-Gil, 2009; Ganter & Hecker, 2013; Kim et al., 2014; Sarooghi et al., 2015; Mabad et al., 2021)	**Recruitment** (Som, 2008; Zheng et al., 2009; Jain et al., 2012; Arar & Öneren, 2018; McCrindle & Fell, 2019; Agarwala et al., 2020; Barhate & Dirani, 2022)	**Open communication** (Booysen, 2007; Sambantham et al., 2016; Park and Doo, 2020)
Firm structure (Cosh et al., 2012; Al-Ansari, 2014; Kim et al., 2014; Kawasaki, 2015)	**Training** (Jain et al., 2012; Joshi et al., 2017; Lukianoff & Haidt, 2019; McCrindle & Fell, 2019; Schroth, 2019; Gabrielova & Buchko, 2021)	**Collaboration** (Davidson & Ferdman, 2002; Roberson, 2006; Hartnell et al., 2019)
Leadership style (Ren et al., 2018; Gabrielova & Buchko, 2021)	**Performance appraisal** (Agarwala, 2003; Jain et al., 2012)	**Flexibility** (Park & Doo, 2020; Booysen, 2007; Sambantham et al., 2016)
Organizational culture (Schein, 1997; Davidson & Ferdman, 2002; Roberson, 2006; Booysen, 2007; Sambantham et al., 2016; Jain et al., 2012; Lin, 2014; Hartnell et al., 2019; Park & Doo, 2020; Zeraatkar et al., 2020; Asfahani et al., 2021)	**Continuous feedback/ Communication** (McCrindle & Fell, 2019; Gabrielova & Buchko, 2021)	**Supportive leadership style** (Ren et al., 2018; Gabrielova & Buchko, 2021)
	Reward and recognition (Zheng et al., 2009; Jain et al., 2012; Agarwala et al., 2020)	

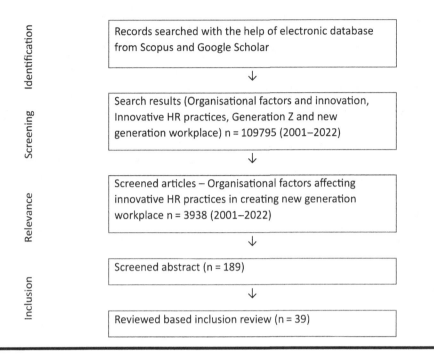

Figure 10.1   Article searching process.

10.3 PRISMA Diagram

10.3.1 Characteristics and Expectations of Generation Z (1997–2012)

Gen Z is more welcoming in nature and open-minded (Gabrielova & Buchko, 2021; Aggarwal et al., 2022; Tagare, 2022). They love to welcome changes and accept challenges and opportunities. This generation is a good initiator and highly ambitious, with a pragmatic approach (Aggarwal et al., 2022). In addition to that, they are good learners and critical thinkers too, which favors digital learning, with YouTube being their preferred learning platform (OECD, 2016). However, research has also claimed that 90% of Gen Z have displayed psychological and physical symptoms due to stress (Bethune, 2019). Of Gen Z, 46% experience stress all or most of the time and burnout, and 75% expect hybrid (offline and remote) working. The massive use of smartphones, social media, and the open social justice movement brought up by the protective parents gives them a sense of safety and quick mood change.

The new generation has unique job expectations and inclinations, which have caught the attention of recent researchers (Ngoc Thang et al., 2022). Researchers have shown that this generation usually values work-life balance, supervisor's continuous feedback, technological and human connection, and a fun-friendly-flexible working environment (Ozkan & Solmaz, 2015; Chillakuri, 2020; Ngoc Thang et al., 2022).

10.4 The Organizational Factor of Innovative HR Practices and New-Generation Workplace

"An organizational innovation is the implementation of a new organizational method in the firm's business practices, workplace organization or external relations" (OECD, 2005, 51). "The Organizational factors are expressed as openness in communication, control mechanisms, environmental scanning intensity, organizational and managerial support, and organizational values" (Antoncic & Hisrich, 2001; Ekingen et al., 2018). Organizational factors (leadership style, organizational structure, organizational cultures, resource utilization in organizations) lead to intrapreneurship (risk-taking, competitive aggressiveness, self-renewal, and autonomy) and service innovation performance. Regarding organizational context, firm-level characteristics like size, workforce education, and geographic reach posit hypotheses on their effects on a firm's propensity to innovate organizationally (Mol & Birkinshaw, 2009; Ganter & Hecker, 2013).

10.4.1 Size of the Organization

Large companies invest more in staffing, training, and development to reduce employee turnover and achieve organizational goals (Kim et al., 2014). Investment in digital recruitment yields a larger pool of suitable candidates at a lesser cost (Hausdorf & Duncan, 2004). Training and development for the organization's employees are to update and grow their competencies and skills to match the current market requirement (Roberson, 2006). As Generation Z expects to upgrade their skills, organizations have initiated outbound training programs to cater for this generation.

Mabad et al. (2021) undertook a study on construction organizations. They found that small-sized organizations, especially those in remote areas, need help adopting and implementing new technologies and achieving success (Tjebane et al., 2022). Unlike smaller organizations, larger organizations can arrange the resources required to adopt new technologies and afford experimentation for innovation. Due to the need for more resources, smaller firms must choose between the options (Damanpour

& Gopalakrishnan, 2001; Naranjo-Gil, 2009). Born and brought up in the technology arena, this new generation frequently updates themselves with new technologies as a basic need (Vickberg & Tankersley, 2023). Sarooghi et al. (2015) mentioned Jackson's (1996) study on how team size affects creativity and innovation. It describes that a larger team size has the benefits of diversity and diversified thoughts and ideas that enhance better decision-making. Sarooghi et al. (2015) considered the size of the team as the size of the organization. Larger companies also have more excellent research capabilities, vast experience in new product or process development, robust marketing capabilities, financial resources and more collaboration with other firms to facilitate innovation (Branzei & Vertinsky, 2006; Sarooghi et al., 2015). Size of the organization yields better process innovation than product innovation (Sarooghi et al., 2015).

Research shows that large-scale operation is highly likely to gain productivity (Damanpour & Schneider, 2006; Ganter & Hecker, 2013). So, the larger organization can afford the cost of implementing innovative practices than the smaller ones (Mol & Birkinshaw, 2009) due to the updated technology adoption (Mabad et al., 2021) and financial resources (Branzei & Vertinsky, 2006) available for investing in various training and development programs to update the knowledge and skills of human resources. Smaller firms should adopt new technologies to attract new generations and benefit from their unique skill set.

10.4.2 Organizational Structure

Cosh et al. (2012) explained organizational structure based on three dimensions; level of centralization, formalization, and integration. According to the researcher, a decentralized structure provides autonomy in decision-making and strategic planning processes. A rigid centralized structure, and a typical top-down approach in formal communication, can hinder the flexibility essential for innovative practices (Al-Ansari, 2014).

Formalization entails that schedules, norms, and rules must be followed, but the employees will have their own choice of work. The formalization must be flexible as it will restrict the freedom to think (Kawasaki, 2015). In his study, Kawasaki (2015) suggests that firms operating in dynamic environments need informal structures to communicate freely, collect information and stay aware of any change. Organizations with decentralized structures with formal approaches are more innovative than others, basically in high-tech industries, considered highly turbulent. This structure is necessary to bring in more staff for involvement in decision-making and strategic planning processes, as knowledge and skills requirement changes frequently in volatile environments (Cosh et al., 2012). Ngoc Thang et al. (2022) discussed in their study that Gen Zers would like a friendly work environment in which rigid and formal structures cannot accommodate them. Organizations with less formalized structures facilitate their employees to communicate freely about their problems, which leads to identifying the training needs (Kim et al., 2014). Effective training programs provided to the employees as per their need leads to job satisfaction and lesser turnover (Kim et al., 2014; Popp et al., 2019; Prilyana & Aseanty, 2020).

A high level of integration is required to create an environment for innovation. Integration refers to the coordination among teams from different departments, open communication and proper technological forum to share knowledge, discuss problems and identify the best suitable solution (Cosh et al., 2012). Gen Zers expect their superior to give continuous feedback and public affirmation and create a friendly, open and emotionally safe environment where they can freely share their ideas (McCrindle & Fell, 2019). Therefore, the challenge in front of HR practitioners remains equally trendy, tech-savvy, and dynamic in using social media, mobile, big data, and cloud (Joshi et al., 2017).

10.4.3 Leadership Style

Ren et al. (2018) studied in China on leadership preferences of Generation Z and found that they prefer highly relationship-oriented leadership styles to work with. This type of leadership style includes participative and coaching leadership. This generation expects mentorship, a positive attitude, and development opportunities from their leaders (Gabrielova & Buchko, 2021). Jayathilake et al. (2021) mentioned in their study that for Generation Z's development and retention, reverse mentorship will mentor the older generation to share their expertise in digital topics, and technology use is the best solution.

10.4.4 Organizational Culture

"The collection of shared, taken-for-granted beliefs that a group possesses and defines how it perceives, thinks about, and responds to its diverse settings" is called organizational culture (Schein, 1997, 236). Involvement, adaptability, mission, and consistency in one organization's culture allow creativity and innovation (Zeraatkar et al., 2020). Employees can commit to the existing organization and be happy if HR practices are well-prepared to provide them with improved and respectful working conditions. While flexible organizational cultures can support HR practices by providing more opportunities for employee development and giving them the autonomy and authority to make decisions, participatory organizational cultures help strengthen HR practices by encouraging teamwork, open communication, and trust, which encourages workers to cooperate to address organizational issues (Davidson & Ferdman, 2002; Roberson, 2006; Hartnell et al., 2019). In a study, Park and Doo (2020) argue that affiliation, open communication and membership support in a firm's culture allow for high-performing HR practices leading to female managers' commitment and satisfaction. In a multicultural organization, to deal with employees from different backgrounds, senior leaders' commitment to devise required change per the organization's vision and communicating the same to the concerned stakeholders is important (Booysen & van Wyk, 2007). An environment that values diversity and inclusion should be reflective of many groups and encourage adaptability and choice (Roberson, 2006).

The new-generation employees believe in maintaining good relationships with their peers. Social interaction and work collaboration are both vital for them. A culture of open communication among employees, which encourages exchanging ideas, must be welcomed (Sambantham & Venkatratnamaraju, 2016). Gen Z wants their ideas recognized and valued (Gabriela & Buchko, 2021). Lin et al. (2014) advocated a network-building HR practice for top management teams to enhance firm performance. Jain et al. (2012) also proposed that employee participation in decision-making can positively influence employees. Asfahani et al. (2021) proposed a "Best Practice Model" that helps the HR management enhance the employees' best practices and helps them fit with the organization's culture.

10.5 HR Practices and New-Generation Workplace

10.5.1 Recruitment

With attracting new-generation employees, the next challenge for the HR practitioner is, recruiting, training, and retaining them employees. Along with the employer branding, the companies must offer a catchy "Employee Value Proposition" (McCrindle & Fell,2019). Gen Z wants a clear and specific reason to join the organization and prefers to grow by exploring multiple job roles (Arar & Öneren, 2018; Barhate & Dirani, 2022). While using the green recruitment process, greater emphasis to be given to recruiting people who are the best fit for the organizational culture (Som, 2008; Zheng et al., 2009; Jain et al., 2012; Agarwala et al., 2020).

10.5.2 Training

Most Gen Z professionals need professional training to remain relevant in the ever-changing industry. They prefer people skills, leadership capabilities, team-building training, and technology (Gaikwad and Pandey 2022). The HR may even arrange outbound training like rock climbing, trekking, and other mental and physical exercises (Jain et al., 2012; McCrindle & Fell,2019). Digital learning is the preferable mode of learning for them. There are organizations which are using massive open online courses (MOOCs) and small private online courses (SPOCs) for their employees' growth and development (Joshi et al., 2017). Upbringing in purely technologically developing and fast-changing surroundings and under minute observation and care (Lukianoff & Haidt, 2019), life skills learning still needs to be fulfilled. The quick burnout and stress of the new generation can be handled rationally by providing soft skills training which will not only help them to reduce stress (Schroth, 2019) and anxiety but also will enhance their self-esteem, time management, confidence, and autonomy (Gabrielova & Buchko, 2021). Jayathilake et al. (2021) argued in their study that to ensure employee development and reduce turnover intention, the role of reverse mentoring, democratizing learning, and intrapreneurship is significant.

10.5.3 Performance Appraisal

This generation complements appraisal, but the weightage should be given to an individual, the team, and organizational performance using quantifiable appraisal criteria (Agarwala, 2003). The organization should maintain a Potential Performance Matrix for each employee. The HR practitioners should prefer an online system for appraisal and can go for Smart Goal Setting and mapping Key Result Area (KRA) (Jain et al., 2012).

10.5.4 Supervisor's Continuous Feedback/Communication

Gen Z always prefers the inspiring, participative leadership style in their workplace. They expect their superior to give continuous feedback, give public affirmation, and create a friendly, open and emotionally safe environment where they can freely share their ideas (McCrindle & Fell, 2019). Therefore, the challenge for HR practitioners is to remain equally trendy, tech-savvy, and dynamic in using social media, mobile, big data, and the cloud (Joshi et al., 2017). Generation Z expects regular feedback, unlike millennials, who seek feedback but hesitate to accept it positively. The delayed response makes them "check out" (Gabrielova & Buchko, 2021; Ruhela & Pandey, 2022).

10.5.5 Reward and Recognition

Gen Z prefers changes, varieties, and challenges. They will only like to stick to an organization if they receive a promotion. It entails a psychological contract (Chakraborty et al., 2023). For them, opportunity for advancement is an essential attribute of a workplace. So, ensuring employee loyalty and commitment towards organizational employment benefits in monetary and non-monetary forms is crucial (Zheng et al., 2009). Therefore, performance-wise awards, cash rewards, rewarding teams for extraordinary performance, public recognition for good performance at company meetings or functions, and recognition from coworkers may be essential HR activities to encourage employee engagement within the organization (Agarwala et al., 2020). Jain et al. (2012) also proposed foreign trips, hard cash, and increasing variable parts of the package as motivation.

10.6 Managerial Implication and Future Scope of Study

Researchers, practitioners, and managers of organizations can get insights into the characteristics of a new generation (Generation Z) and their expectations of the organization. Managers can be aware of the organizational factors, viz. size, structure, leadership style, and culture requirement of one organization to create a suitable workplace for a new generation. They can also get insights about optimizing Generation Z's unique skills to achieve the organizational goal.

Though the study has explored the organizational factors responsible for creating innovative HR practices, it has some limitations. The study has considered journal articles from limited databases. The possibility of not including other forms of studies and the relevant papers available in other databases might be there.

Though the current study has focused on only the organizational factor responsible for creating innovative HR practices, studies can be done on exploring other possible factors related to this. The proposed model can be tested using qualitative or quantitative approaches in different organizations to prove its applicability in various sectors.

10.7 Conclusion

Considering the characteristics of Generation Z, organizations are suggested to adjust their system to create a suitable workplace. HR systems and practices should have innovativeness to optimize the skills of the new generation to achieve organizational goals. The organizational factor is the prime determinant that can facilitate innovation in the firm. Many pieces of evidence in research indicate that the size of the firm, structure, and organizational culture are the subsets of organizational factors. The firm's size highly impacts innovation. Larger organizations have more potential to innovate and implement new practices than smaller organizations. The main reasons for innovation are the large-scale operation, access to a more extensive financial base, and affordability to risk-taking and experimentation.

On the other hand, smaller organizations, though unwillingly, needed more resources to afford experimentation and innovation. Studies also found that a firm's decentralized and less formal structure encourages openness to communication, participation in decision-making, and training need identification that ensures job satisfaction, continuous motivation, and reduced turnover intention. Generation Z requires a culture of open communication, collaboration to work, flexibility, and top management support. This type of culture encourages managers to create network-building HR practices (Lin et al., 2014; Pandey et al., 2021), a best practice model (Asfahani, 2021), and a set of practices which will be best suitable for creating a workplace for a new generation. The conceptual model (Figure 10.2) depicts the findings.

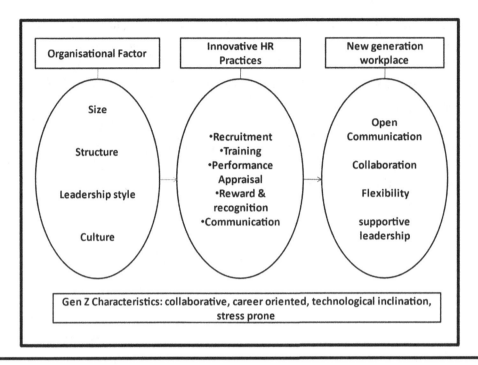

Figure 10.2 Conceptual framework of organizational factor, innovative HR practices, and new-generation workplace.

References

Adecco (2016). Generation Z vs. Millennials. Documentoelectrónicoenlínea: disponible en. https://www.adeccousa.com/employers/resources/generation-z-vs-millennials-infographic/.

Agarwala, T. (2003). Innovative human resource practices and organizational commitment: An empirical investigation. *International Journal of Human Resource Management, 14*(2), 175–197.

Agarwala, T., Arizkuren, A., Del Castillo, E., & Muniz, M. (2020). Work–family culture and organizational commitment: A multidimensional cross-national study. *Personnel Review, 49*(7), 1467–1486.

Aggarwal, A., Sadhna, P., Gupta, S., Mittal, A., & Rastogi, S. (2022). Gen z entering the workforce: Restructuring HR policies and practices for fostering the task performance and organizational commitment. *Journal of Public Affairs, 22*(3), e2535.

Al-Ansari, Y. D. Y. (2014). *Innovation practices as a path to business growth performance: a study of small and medium-sized firms in the emerging UAE market* (Doctoral dissertation, Southern Cross University).

Antoncic, B., & Hisrich, R. D. (2001). Intrapreneurship: Construct refinement and cross-cultural validation. *Journal of Business Venturing, 16*(5), 495–527.

Arar, T., & Öneren, M. (2018). Role of talent management in the career development of Generation Z: A case study of a telecommunication firm. *International Academic Journal of Social Sciences, 5*(1), 28–44.

Asfahani, A. (2021). The impact of modern strategic human resources management models on promoting organizational agility. *Academy of Strategic Management Journal, 20*(2), 1–11.

Barhate, B., & Dirani, K. M. (2022). Career aspirations of Generation Z: A systematic literature review. *European Journal of Training and Development, 46*(1/2), 139–157.

Bencsik, A., Horváth-Csikós, G., & Juhász, T. (2016). Y and Z Generations at workplaces. *Journal of Competitiveness, 8*(3), 90–106.

Bethune, S. (2019). Gen Z is more likely to report mental health concerns. *American Psychological Association.* https://www.apa.org/monitor/2019/01/gen-z

Booysen, L. A., & van Wyk, M. W. (2007). Culture and leadership in South Africa. In *Culture and Leadership Across the World* (pp. 467–508). Psychology Press.

Branzei, O., & Vertinsky, I. (2006). Strategic pathways to product innovation capabilities in SMEs. *Journal of Business Venturing, 21*(1), 75–105.

Chakraborty, S., Pandey, S., & Khurana, A. (2023). Psychological contract types influence on innovative work behaviour: Mediating role of leader–member exchange in service sector during pandemic. *FIIB Business Review.* https://doi.org/10.1177/23197145231156072

Chaudhary, R. (2020). Green human resource management and green employee behaviour: An empirical analysis. *Corporate Social Responsibility and Environmental Management, 27*(2), 630–641.

Chillakuri, B. (2020). Understanding Generation Z expectations for effective onboarding. *Journal of Organizational Change Management, 33*(7), 1277–1296.

Collins, C. J., & Clark, K. D. (2003). Strategic human resource practices, top management team social networks, and firm performance: The role of human resource practices in creating organizational competitive advantage. *Academy of Management Journal, 46*(6), 740–751.

Cosh, A., Fu, X., & Hughes, A. (2012). Organization structure and innovation performance in different environments. *Small Business Economics, 39*, 301–317.

Damanpour, F., & Gopalakrishnan, S. (2001). The dynamics of the adoption of product and process innovations in organizations. *Journal of Management Studies, 38*(1), 45–65.

Damanpour, F., & Schneider, M. (2006). Phases of the adoption of innovation in organizations: Effects of environment, organization and top managers 1. *British Journal of Management, 17*(3), 215–236.

Davidson, M. N., & Ferdman, B. M. (2002). Inclusion and power: Reflections on dominance and subordination in organizations. *The Industrial-Organizational Psychologist, 40*(1), 62–67.

Ekingen, E., Ekemen, M. A., Yildiz, A., & Korkmazer, F. (2018). The effect of intrapreneurship and organizational factors on the innovation performance in hospitals. *Revista de Cercetaresi Interventie Sociala, 62*, 196.

Gabrielova, K., & Buchko, A. A. (2021). Here comes Generation Z: Millennials as managers. *Business Horizons, 64*(4), 489–499.

Gaikwad, P., & Pandey, S. (2022) A review on Special Skill Sets from Industry 4.0 Perspective. Proceedings - 2022 2nd International Conference on Electronic and Electrical Engineering and Intelligent System, ICE3IS, 276–281.

Ganter, A., & Hecker, A. (2013). Deciphering antecedents of organizational innovation. *Journal of Business Research, 66*(5), 575–584.

Gardner, T. M., Moynihan, L. M., Park, H. J., & Wright, P. M. (2001). Beginning to unlock the black box in the HR firm performance relationship: The impact of HR practices on employee attitudes and employee outcomes.

Global Talent (2022, May). *Deloitte*. The mental health of Gen Zs and millennials in the new world of work. https://www2.deloitte.com/content/dam/Deloitte/global/Documents/deloitte-2022-genz-millennial-mh-whitepaper.pdf

Grow, J. M., & Yang, S. (2018). Generation Z enters the advertising workplace: Expectations through a gendered lens. *Journal of Advertising Education, 22*(1), 7–22.

Hartnell, C. A., Ou, A. Y., Kinicki, A. J., Choi, D., & Karam, E. P. (2019). A meta-analytic test of organizational culture's association with an organization's system elements and its relative predictive validity on organizational outcomes. *Journal of Applied Psychology, 104*(6), 832.

Hausdorf, P. A., & Duncan, D. (2004). Firm size and Internet recruiting in Canada: A preliminary investigation. *Journal of Small Business Management, 42*(3), 325–334.

Jackson, S. E. (1996). The consequences of diversity in multidisciplinary work teams. *Handbook of Work Group Psychology*, 53–75.

Jain, H., Mathew, M., & Bedi, A. (2012). HRM innovations by Indian and foreign MNCs operating in India: A survey of HR professionals. *The International Journal of Human Resource Management, 23*(5), 1006–1018.

Jayathilake, H. D., Daud, D., Eaw, H. C., & Annuar, N. (2021). Employee development and retention of Generation-Z employees in the post-COVID-19 workplace: A conceptual framework. *Benchmarking: An International Journal, 28*(7), 2343–2364.

Joshi, A., Sunny, N., & Vashisht, S. (2017). Recent trends in HRM: A qualitative analysis using AHP. *Prabandhan: Indian Journal of Management, 10*(10), 41–52.

Kawasaki, R. (2015). Determinants of innovation performance: A resource-based study. *Procedia-Social and Behavioral Sciences, 195*, 1330–1337.

Kehoe, R. R., & Wright, P. M. (2013). The impact of high-performance human resource practices on employees' attitudes and behaviours. *Journal of Management, 39*(2), 366–391.

Khatri, N., & Budhwar, P. S. (2002). A study of strategic HR issues in an Asian context. *Personnel Review, 31*(2), 166–188.

Kim, Y. H., Sting, F. J., & Loch, C. H. (2014). Top-down, bottom-up, or both? Toward an integrative perspective on operations strategy formation. *Journal of Operations Management, 32*(7–8), 462–474.

Lin, Y., Zhao, S., & Li, N. (2014). A study of network-building HR practices for TMT, strategic flexibility and firm performance: The moderating role of environmental uncertainty. *Nankai Business Review International, 5*(1), 95–114.

Lukianoff, G., & Haidt, J. (2019). *The Coddling of the American Mind: How Good Intentions and Bad Ideas Are Setting up a Generation for Failure*. Newyork: Penguin.

Mabad, T., Ali, O., Ally, M., Wamba, S. F., & Chan, K. C. (2021). Making investment decisions on RFID technology: An evaluation of key adoption factors in construction firms. *IEEE Access, 9*, 36937–36954.

McCrindle, M., & Fell, A. (2019). *Understanding Generation Z: Recruiting, Training and Leading the Next Generation.* Australia: McCrindle Research Pty Ltd.

Moher, D., Liberati, A., Tetzlaff, J., & Altman, D. G. (2009). Preferred reporting items for systematic reviews and meta-analyses: The PRISMA statement. *Journal of Clinical Epidemiology, 62*(10), 1006–1012. http://doi.org/10.1016/j.jclinepi.2009.06.005

Mol, M. J., & Birkinshaw, J. (2009). The sources of management innovation: When firms introduce new management practices. *Journal of Business Research, 62*(12), 1269–1280.

Naranjo-Gil, D. (2009). The influence of environmental and organizational factors on innovation adoptions: Consequences for performance in public sector organizations. *Technovation, 29*(12), 810–818.

Ngoc Thang, N., Rowley, C., Mayrhofer, W., & Anh, N. T. P. (2022). Generation Z job seekers in Vietnam: CSR-based employer attractiveness and job pursuit intention. *Asia Pacific Business Review*, 1–19.

OECD. (2016). *Innovating Education and Educating for Innovation: The Power of Digital Technologies and Skills*, Paris: OECD. http://doi.org/10.1787/9789264265097-en

OECD/Eurostat. (2005). *Oslo Manual, Guidelines for Collecting and Interpreting Innovation Data*, Paris: OECD.

Ozkan, M., & Solmaz, B. (2015). The changing faces of the employees–generation Z and their perceptions of work (a study applied to university students). *Procedia Economics and Finance, 26*, 476–483.

Palomo, J., Figueroa-Domecq, C., & Laguna, P. (2017). Women, peace and security state-of-art: A bibliometric analysis in social sciences based on SCOPUS database. *Scientometrics* 113, 123–148. https://doi.org/10.1007/s11192-017-2484-x

Pandey, S., Ruhela, V., & Ruhela, S. (2021). Precursors and ramifications of creativity on innovation in product design teams-a study on Indian information technology sector. *Journal of Physics: Conference Series, 1860*(1), 012014.

Park, S., & Doo, M. Y. (2020). The effect of organizational culture and HR practices on female managers' commitment and job satisfaction. *European Journal of Training and Development, 44* (2/3), 105–120.

Popp, N., Simmons, J., & Mc Evoy, C. (2019). Effects of employee training on job satisfaction outcomes among sport ticket sellers. *International Journal of Sport Management and Marketing, 19*(3–4), 147–160.

Prilyana, C., & Aseanty, D. (2020). The effect of training satisfaction to turnover intention mediated by organizational citizenship behavior and job satisfaction in employees of bank Syariah in Jakarta. *Webology, 17*(2), 551–567.

Ramkumar, A., & Rajini, G. (2018). Innovative human resource practices and selected HR outcomes in software firms. *International Journal of Innovation, Creativity and Change, 4*(2), 134–157.

Ren, S., Xie, Y., Zhu, Y., & Warner, M. (2018). New generation employees' preferences towards leadership style in China. *Asia Pacific Business Review*, *24*(4), 437–458.

Roberson, Q. M. (2006). Disentangling the meanings of diversity and inclusion in organizations. *Group & Organization Management*, *31*(2), 212–236.

Ruhela, V., & Pandey, S. (2022). Emotional intelligence, conflict management styles and innovative work behaviour - a study on Indian employees. *International Journal of Early Childhood Special Education*, *14*(4), 2678–2684.

Sambantham, M., & Venkatratnamaraju, D. (2016). Human resources management (HRM) practices in multinational companies. *International Journal of Pharmacy and Technology*, *8*(3), 15516–15522.

Sarooghi, H., Libaers, D., & Burkemper, A. (2015). Examining the relationship between creativity and innovation: A meta-analysis of organizational, cultural, and environmental factors. *Journal of Business Venturing*, *30*(5), 714–731.

Schein, E. H. (1997). *Organizational Culture and Leadership* (2nd ed.). San Francisco: Jossey Bass.

Schroth, H. (2019). Are you ready for Gen Z in the workplace? *California Management Review*, *61*(3), 5–18.

Som, A. (2008). Innovative human resource management and corporate performance in the context of economic liberalisation in India. *The International Journal of Human Resource Management*, *19*(7), 1278–1297.

Staglin, G. (2022, January 22). The future of work depends on supporting Gen Z. *Forbes*. https://www.forbes.com/sites/onemind/2022/07/22/the-future-of-work-depends-on-supporting-gen-z/?sh=7bde173447af

Tagare, R. Jr. (2022). An ethnographic probe on the cultural values and symbols of Generation Z students: Implications for course contextualisation. *European Online Journal of Natural and Social Sciences*, *11*(2), 347.

Tjebane, M. M., Musonda, I., & Okoro, C. (2022). Organizational factors of artificial intelligence adoption in the South African construction industry. *Frontiers in Built Environment*, *8*, 823998.

Turner, A. (2015). Generation Z: Technology and social interest. *The Journal of Individual Psychology*, *71*(2), 103–113.

Vickberg, S., & Tankersley, J. (2023, January 30). Help me grow! What motivates Gen Z? *Deloitte*. https://www2.deloitte.com/us/en/blog/business-chemistry/2023/help-me-grow-what-motivates-gen-z.html

Zeraatkar, M., Roudneshin, M., & Sobhanallahi, M. A. (2020). The effect of organizational culture on creativity and innovation processes (case study: Tondar Department of IKCO). *International Journal of Business Information Systems*, *33*(1), 80–102.

Zheng, C., O'Neill, G., & Morrison, M. (2009). Enhancing Chinese SME performance through innovative HR practices. *Personnel Review*, *38*(2), 175–194.

Chapter 11

Disengagement to Engagement: A Strategic Employee Retention Approach with AI

Sankar Mukherjee
GIBS Business School, Bangaluru, India

Poorvi Agrawal
Galgotias University, Greater Noida, India

11.1 Introduction

The word "Employee Retention" has been the most challenging job the human resources (HR) department faces for an extended period of time. It has become a more daunting responsibility for HR to retain employees than to onboard employees. The employee turnover ratio is the most potential threat to any organization. It is more predominant in skilled industries like IT (Gaikwad & Pandey 2022; Kamble & Pandey 2022), ITES, education, and consulting firms. People are considered a volatile asset. So human beings are also considered as capital. Hence, nurturing human capital and retaining them is one of the most intuitive tasks for any HR department. Technological adoption in strategic human resource management (SHRM) makes HR operations more transparent and robust. HR policy mechanism integrates with technology to take strategic decision. Adopting artificial intelligence (AI) is a way forward in this direction. The cost of recruiting the right talent impounds more risk to the organization if the talent leaves the organization within a short period. Technology intervention is a way forward to arrest the attrition issue considered by many industry experts with acquisition as a beginning step (Pandey & Bahukhandi 2022). A recent study revealed that 52% of employees could have been prevented from leaving the company if timely analysis of their issues with data (Wiles 2021) in Gartner, article. The former CEO of IBM has expressed confidence in a pilot program initiated by his company almost to predict 95% accuracy to identify the selected employees who could quit their job (Rosenbaum 2019). So, amid the talent retention war, a question is hovering around the air: Can technology, particularly AI, help prevent the employee from resigning by supplying the correct data to take timely decisions to curb attrition?

11.2 Understanding Artificial Intelligence (AI)

Unfortunately, there is no fixed definition of AI. Many researchers have defined AI in their own ways. So, despite different shared definitions, it is considered the replacement of human intelligence artificially made based on the algorithm. The most basic nature of AI is to drive the decision based on multiple computing and analysis supported by programme-based algorithms. Different types of AI aim to function the array of multiple functions in the divergent areas where the human brain exercises the capabilities. AI as a rational computing ability is considered a weak AI. Other types of AI are called strong AIs that cater to human-like capabilities. Weak AI is the base where a pool of data is being analysed. The next step is machine learning (ML), where AI learns by itself through data and algorithms to meet the accuracy of decision-making. The next phase is deep learning (DL), considered the sub-set of ML based on artificial neural networks (ANNs).

11.3 Strategic Change in Human Resource Management: An Adoption of AI

The evolution and change of human resource management (HRM) have transformed into SHRM. The changes in business decision-making have considerably shifted from perspective-based decision-making to data-based decision-making across all business domains. The evolution has occurred with the advent of technology and its quick adoption. The organization intends to decide with more accuracy based on data. Technology plays a catalyst role in making decisions more precisely that have not been executed in the past. So, adopting technology became necessary for all organizations across all domains.

Under the perspective of holistic changes in the business economy globally, HR adopts a strategic shift from HRM to human resource strategic management (HRSM).

11.3.1 *Pictorial Presentation of AI in Employee Engagement and Retention*

As per the strategic HR theory, HR strategy must be coined with business strategy (Baird & Meshoulam 1988; Wright & Snell 1998). So, AI has started integrating with strategic HR functions recently (Figure 11.1). Previous studies posit that AI in HRM as a human–computer interaction ensures more management efficiency in decisions (Bhardwaj, Singh, & Kumar 2020) through the collection, maintenance, and validation of data of employees. To make it more precise HRM transforms into data-driven decision-making based on analysis in talent acquisition (TA), training, performance

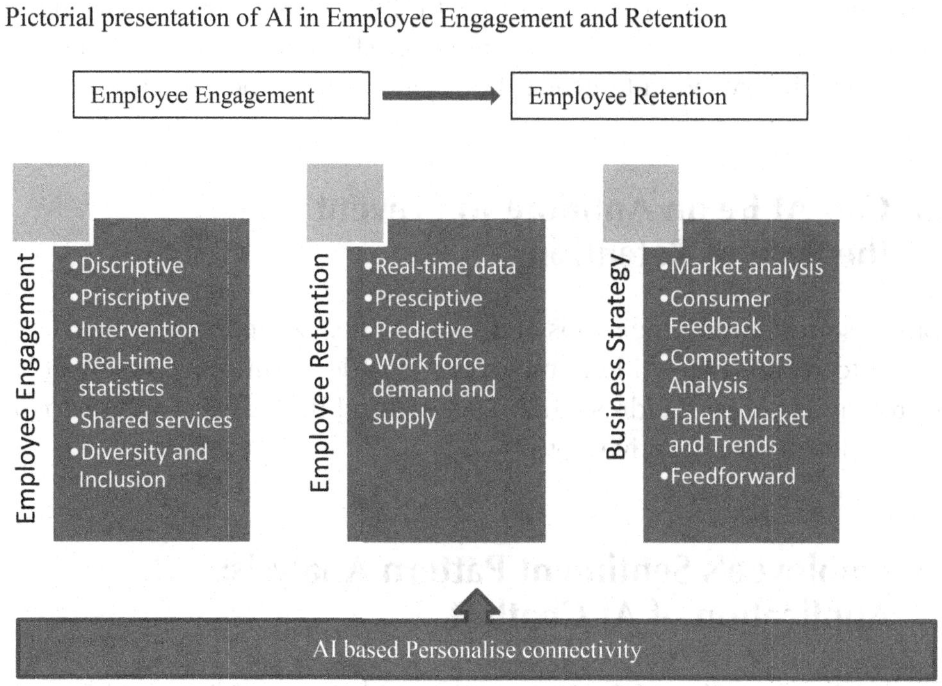

Pictorial presentation of AI in Employee Engagement and Retention

Figure 11.1   AI in Employee engagement and retention.

management, performance appraisal system, and retention management. But, the application of AI in HRM is still in a nascent state, as many areas of HR have not been explored (Pandey & Khaskel 2019).

11.4 Employee Retention: The Formidable Challenge

In the current competitive business environment, the most formidable challenge faced by HR is nothing but the retention of employees. There are a plethora of reasons that employees quit the organization. It is becoming more apparent in the competitive environment, as skill resources always find an opportunity to migrate from one place to another. However, from the organization's point of view, it is the most concerning area as the cost of TA soars up if the attrition rate goes up. There are a few business sectors like IT, ITES, and research and development (R&D); education is among few areas where retention of skilled resources is the most daunting task that today's HRM confronts. A recent report has shown that the pace of employee turnover will surpass over 50–75%, as forecasted earlier (Wiles, 2021). The lack of career progression is still considered the most common reason for quitting the job. On the contrary, 65% of employees are investigating the role of current jobs in their lives. Hence, assuming the situation under this complex perspective, HR managers are in quest of technological intervention to arrest the retention rate under their control.

11.5 Can AI Be an Antidote to Prevent the Rate of Retention?

Employees are quitting their jobs at a record rate. Companies are in a dilemma to retain their skilled employees in order to improve turnover ratio and profitability. Can I address the issues behind the scene? Let us explore the possibilities on a positive note.

11.6 Employee's Sentiment Pattern Analysis: Application of AI Chatbot

According to a recent report, most employees leave their boss, not the organization (McKinsey, March 2022). Uncaring leadership is the core reason. Being unable to connect with empathy is crucial for showing uncaring behaviour towards colleagues. If employees' sentiments and involvement can be assessed, most of these problems could be sorted out. More recently, a few companies like KPMG have adopted an interactive chatbot to understand the pulse of the sentiment of their employees. The result is encouraging as KPMG claims that two-thirds of their employees come under their scanner as probable employees to leave the organization soon. A subsequent step was taken to prevent the 10–20% resignation.

11.7 Employee's Mood Analysis: Role of Chatbot

A chatbot called Amber, introduced by GENPACT, has successfully predicted the mood of their employees to understand the state of happiness and unhappiness. The score has been developed with the data and takes preventive action assuming the low mood score is a critical indicator for the employee to leave the organization soon.

11.8 Augmented Human Resource: Intervention of AI to Prevent Attrition

The intervention of AI to manage retention is called augmented HR. A recent study has revealed a surging demand for more spending on augmented HR (Kaur & Kaur 2022). It has grown by leaps in the last year and is projected to reach $766 billion in 2025 (Globenewswire 2021).

A recent research-based study showed that over 50% of large-scale organizations are in the phase of implementation of AI-related tools to the multi-layers of HR functions (Eightfold AI 2021). Notably, most companies are deeply involved in promoting the mechanism of AI-based recruitment and training processes. This is the first step to the part of strategic retention policy, as recruiting the potential candidate for the right kind of KRAs (Key Responsible Areas) helps to slow down the activity of quitting the company by providing job satisfaction. The study further released a fascinating report that more than 82% of large-scale companies plan to roll out AI in their SHRM within five years.

11.9 Flight-Risk Employees: AI as an Identifier

Identifying disengaged employees is the first step to churn and control employees' risk movement. It is a more herculean task for large organizations to spot the warning sign. This is where AI can nip the prospect of leaving the organization's employees in the bud. Following are the initial strategies that companies can endorse to have control of retention from the very beginning.

11.10 Career Planning: The Role of AI to Engage

Employee engagement is another area of threat to employee turnover. Now, companies are converging their organizational behaviour approach towards more employees centric.

Understanding employee behavioural psychology with data is the core area in AI that can play a significant role. AI-powered technology ensures a personalized approach to understanding the needs of individual employees and makes tailored solutions for their careers.

11.11 Talent Nourishment: Solution through AI-Driven Training and Learning

Stagnation in career growth is one of the major concerns for employees. Human skill is volatile, particularly in the domain of soft skill drive assignment. Skills and talent are in rising demand. Employer and employees both value skills and prepared for based work norms. As per the study, more than 60% of employees needed help finding a creative environment to develop their skills and competencies Cantrell, Griffiths, Jones & Hiipakka (2022). Moreover, many researchers have found that the lion's share of employees believe that state-of-the-art training with simulation in training can increase skills and reskill their productivity. AI-based software leverages the opportunity of customized learning experiences to make employees more engaged with the company. Hence, attrition can be under control.

11.12 The Strategy of Succession Planning: A Silver Line for the Future with AI

Customized training and learning approaches are paving the path to identifying the right talent for the company in future. Succession planning is one of the grey areas for most companies nowadays. Moreover, project-based IT software companies must build their future reserve bench for leaders under strategic succession planning. AI-oriented software makes it more focused on data-driven analysis. Customized data from individual employees ensure to find out the skills and competencies of the employee to groom them as future leaders for the company.

11.13 AI to Solve Conflict Management: The Issue of Excessive Overtime and Attrition

The amount of overtime and non-flexible work options are the primary cause of employee retention. Research shows that workplace flexibility and innovation like work make employees more inclined towards work, which in turn brings sentential productivity (Pandey, Ruhela & Ruhela 2021). AI helps to track that data and makes predictive analysis with transparent communication with employees in obtaining the data and imposing more trust in the culture of any organization (Chakraborty, Pandey & Khurana 2023). The tech giant IBM has successfully brought the conflict under the internal locus of control to prevent the retention from out-of-control. CNBC article from Rosenbaum (2019) mentioned the predictive analysis in program of IBM, backed by AI, named Watson, has exhibited its enormous capability with an accuracy rate of 95% to identify individual employees who are supposed to leave within six months. Real-time action based on AI-driven predictive "attrition program" turns out to be a very successful strategy for HRM.

11.14 Conclusion: A Road Ahead with AI

AI has an extensive and decisive role in arresting the attrition rate. Expert across the business fraternity have expressed their satisfaction that data-driven predictive analysis, through AI, can be the game changer in SHRM. TA, training and learning (T&L), cultural fit, compensation management, performance appraisal system, employee engagement, and retention are the significant areas in HR that can be analysed by AI, and decisions can be taken more accurately. AI has its limitations also in terms of collecting data transparently. However, a study found that employees consent to share their data if the organization reveals the purpose truthfully. Data-driven predictive analysis can make HRM more strategic in developing an employee-centric culture to bring the best from the employees that, in turn, will provide more profitability with an image makeover for any organization.

References

Baird, L., & Meshoulam, I. (1988). Managing two fits of strategic human resource management. *Academy of Management Review*, *13*(1), 116–128.

Bhardwaj, G., Singh, S.V., & Kumar, V. (2020). An Empirical Study of Artificial Intelligence and Its Impact on Human Resource Functions. *2020 International Conference on Computation, Automation and Knowledge Management (ICCAKM)*, 47–51.

Cantrell, S., Griffiths, M., Jones, R., Hiipakka, J. (2022). Deloitte Insights, The skills-based organization: A new operating model for work and the workforce (https://www2.deloitte.com/us/en/insights/topics/talent/organizational-skill-based-hiring.html)

Chakraborty, S., Pandey, S., & Khurana, A. (2023). Psychological contract types influence on innovative work behaviour: Mediating role of leader–member exchange in service sector during pandemic. *FIIB Business Review*. http://doi.org/10.1177/23197145231156072

Eightfold. AI, 2021 HR's Future State Report 2021: The Impact of Artificial Intelligence on Talent Processes (https://eightfold.ai/wp-content/uploads/HR_Future_State_Report_2021.pdf)

Gaikwad, P., & Pandey, S. (2022). A Review on Special Skill Sets from Industry 4.0 Perspective. *Proceedings - 2022 2nd International Conference on Electronic and Electrical Engineering and Intelligent System (ICE3IS)*, 276–281.

GlobeNewswire Market Research Future. (2021). www.globenewswire.com/en/news-release/2021/07/22/2267620/0/en/AR-and-VR-Market-to-Hit-USD-766-Billion-by-2025-Registering-a-73-7-CAGR-Report-by-Market-Research-Future-MRFR.html

Kamble, S., & Pandey, S. (2022). Perception gap analysis of "Employability" amongst academia, IT-industry and fresh engineering graduates. *ECS Transactions*, *107*(1), 10857–10864.

Kaur, R., & Kaur, H. (2022). Predominant Role of Artificial Intelligence in Employee Retention. *Intelligent System Design: Proceedings of INDIA 2022*, 535–546.

Mckinsey Quaterly. (2022). https://www.mckinsey.com/capabilities/people-and-organizational-performance/our-insights/gone-for-now-or-gone-for-good-how-to-play-the-new-talent-game-and-win-back-workers

Pandey, S., & Bahukhandi, M. (2022). Applicants' Perception Towards the Application of AI in Recruitment Process. *2022 International Conference on Interdisciplinary Research in Technology and Management, IRTM 2022*.

Pandey, S., & Khaskel, P. (2019). Application of AI in human resource management and Gen Y's reaction. *International Journal of Recent Technology and Engineering (IJRTE)*, *8*(4), 10325–10331.

Pandey, S., Ruhela, V., & Ruhela, S. (2021). Precursors and ramifications of creativity on innovation in product design teams-a study on Indian information technology sector. *Journal of Physics: Conference Series*, *1860*(1), 012014.

Rosenbaum, E. (2019). CNBC work. www.cnbc.com/2019/04/03/ibm-ai-can-predict-with-95-percent-accuracy-which-employees-will-quit.html

Wiles, J. (2021). Great resignation or not, money won't fix all your talent problems. www.gartner.com/en/articles/great-resignation-or-not-money-won-t-fix-all-your-talent-problems

Wright, P.M., & Snell, S.A. (1998). Toward a unifying framework for exploring fit and flexibility in strategic human resource management. *Academy of Management Review, 23*(4), 756–772.

Chapter 12

HR Transformation and Resiliency

Kashish Ohri and Suruchi Pandey

Symbiosis Institute of Management Studies, Pune, India

12.1 Introduction

The search for meaning in life for individuals is essential. With innumerable uncertainties and circumstances, employees need to buffer themselves better in order to deal with whatever situations come their way. Instead of resigning from the workplaces, they should be able to overcome the challenging conditions and not leave their workplaces for petty troubles. However, little is known about the coping mechanism of being resilient in order to overcome situations in life. When the world was grappling with the COVID-19 pandemic, it was imperative to see here that all of us as individuals were resilient enough to keep working and not leave their workplaces despite facing a deadly pandemic. It is now that we see that employees are coping in a better way with situations post the pandemic since the perspectives have changed, things are seen optimistically and employees are able to cope with fast-paced changes while maintaining a positive work environment. As it is also researched over the years, organizational effectiveness and survival depend hugely on how resilient the organization is since employees, if resilient, are able to adapt and cope well with challenges coming along their way, thereby making organizations successful in the longer run. The need to study this subject through this research paper is that this stems from how organizational structure can be strengthened and

DOI: 10.4324/9781003372622-12

how employees can cope effectively with situations like a pandemic or increased work pressure in today's times. In the current era, wherein work-life balance is of utmost importance, it is imperative to understand how the work environment affects employees' personal lives and how they keep up with taxing situations with a coping mechanism like 'resilience' in today's world.

12.1.1 Resilience at a Glance

Resilience is described as an individual characteristic which ensures that people timely adapt to adversity and can be measured using variables like optimism or health outcome indicators like overall well-being. Studying organizational resilience and employee resilience, both are needed in consonance with each other and thereby, employee resilience means behavioural capability, supported by the organization which reflects the resources being used optimally and also abilities to continually adapt at the workplace and understanding the work pressures. Being resilient comprises of proactive, support-seeking, learning and crisis management behaviours which are developed over a period of time and act as coping mechanisms (Näswall et al., 2019). The ability to bounce back from adversity and even thrive in the face of it is essential but not only what being resilient means. It also includes a preparedness factor which supports crisis management ensuring organizational survival – thereby also being inclusive of proactive and learning behaviours which facilitate change and innovation in the longer run, at the same time supporting employee well-being (Pandey, Ruhela, & Ruhela, 2021). It is a relatively stable personality trait because of which employees can easily overcome setbacks or difficulties and it helps the organizational effectiveness and productivity since even in the face of any hardship, employees always get back up, not hampering the work environment and adapting to the daily routine easily.

12.1.2 Resiliency at the Workplace

In this global era of today, wherein the economies are unstable every step of the way, it is essential that employees need to be ready to face pressures at their workplace. Various setbacks in terms of high- or low-impact events have the potential to impair employee performance at various levels however, which is where workplace resilience comes in the picture.

Workplace resilience essentially means the employees' ability to manage as well as overcome any type of adversity at work, thereby not affecting employee productivity with the organization (Hartwig et al., 2020). Resilience is an important key element in maintaining employee performance and well-being even in the face of adversity. Workplace resiliency has not only been studied by researchers at an individual level but also at a team level as well. In organizations, when most of the work is done in teams, enhancing resilience at a team level is as important as enhancing it as an individual level. At a team level, it means managing the adversities or pressures that the team faces as a whole and coming back even stronger with the capability to deal with such pressures. A team may face mutual challenges and thus it is imperative that there is a collective response to such challenges like a vision towards the same goal or target which also helps the team to be resilient not just on their own but for the team as one unit. What is often misunderstood in this field is that a team of resilient members may not necessarily mean high performance or high productivity, it may still result in poor team performance due to the lack of communication or support within the team or from the top supervisors or management. It is important that various team interactions in the workplace are seen at different levels since that will determine if people are resilient individually or will they also be able to handle adversities in a group since that is what mainly determines the workplace-team productivity and efficiency and the ability to hold a firm ground even if there are various pressures in the workplace. The more resilient an organization is at the macro level, the more it will be able to secure and develop resources for its employees and thereby be successful even in the face of hardships and will be able to recover from various setbacks at a faster pace.

12.1.3 HR Transformation and Resiliency

According to research and studies done before on this topic, it has been seen that when employees see their organization as committed to their overall well-being and health, they all tend to develop a positive outlook or positive psychological links, which in the long run tend to yield positive results and this itself implies that human resource (HR) transformation today plays a significant role in developing positive employee perceptions towards a job which might seem taxing to employees. With respect to this, employee resilience improves their strength to tackle challenges and a myriad of job issues or issues like a pandemic, a financial crisis, etc. thereby reducing the negative mental, physical, and emotional impacts on employees (Amir & Standen, 2019). It enhances their overall mental and physical health since the job seems less demanding and together employees feel that it is easier to cope with the ongoing issue or problem which the organization is facing (Ruhela & Pandey, 2022).

However, in today's global era, what organizations also need is a resilient HR wherein the operating model has to be aligned with the changing needs and situations. In order to cope with these unprecedented times, organizations that are fast, adaptive, and easy to change will have to be built and they will be able to gear themselves for any situation in the future which might be taxing for all employees of the organization and the organization as a whole. This in turn can only be done if there is a resilient HR team present who is able to formulate or devise an action plan which is easy to follow and which has the ability to change at a faster pace with the situations that arise, thereby facing all adversities yet not losing the essence of the organization's mission and objectives for the longer term (Pandey, Ruhela, & Ruhela, 2021; Chakraborty, Pandey, & Khurana, 2023). With this, an organization can build a resilient workforce and will be better positioned to successfully adapt to change, adversities, and challenges in the long run.

When the whole world was battling a pandemic like Covid-19, the employees of each company also had a lot at stake and they were constantly adapting to their surroundings, be it online, offline, or hybrid mode of work. All this was possible because of the modern model that has been adopted by a majority of the organizations which is, react, respond, return, and transform (Avey, Newman, & Herbert, 2022). In the first phase, i.e. react, there were various support leaders assigned to a group of employees; employees were continuously reminded of the mission and objectives of the company, goal was to accomplish small tasks at hand and thereafter achieve huge milestones and finally they were shown a way of optimism and future, a way of making them resilient in such tough times – a time which might arise in the future also and then they are ready in even a better way to react to this. The second phase entailed educating them about the virus, establishing proper communication channels, mandatory leaves, check-ins, and counselling on how to deal with stress and the whole pandemic as well, a proper work-life balance had to be maintained during this time since health was of primary importance but, work at hand could also not afford to come to a halt (Hiebert, 2014). Thereby, after reacting to such a situation in a resilient manner, employees slowly responded to it positively and focused on the bright side where they could spend time with family, manage an apt work-life balance, and take proper care of their health as well but at the same time not compromising on the company's mission and objectives as well. The first two phases were relatively more stressful and employees had to be resilient in such times. If they had not been resilient enough in organizations, the economy would not have pulled back up with such a throttle like it has. The third and fourth phases ran parallel to each other since it was a time when employees were returning back to work in a usual way, however, organizations were operating in new ways and techniques and were ready to tackle any pandemic of the future as well. The business models have been reinvented and employee-customer experience has been rethought of in this phase. Organization missions, goals and missions have been aligned in such a manner that employees have learnt to be resilient in the face of any challenging situation and adapt to an entirely new way of functioning in their respective domains (Rees et al., 2015).

In order to deal with the pandemic and at the same time, plan for the future the whole operating model of HR had to undergo a transformational change in various aspects. HR teams that were efficient, responsive, and resilient enough to tackle such kinds of situations had to be built and this has been for the positive since companies have only enhanced each experience by building such a mix of teams. A big reset for HR was seen known as the resilient HR – which essentially enabled and empowered local HR and other facility teams to act in a crisis like this. Earlier, organizations had multiple programs to train employees, however now the focus has shifted to training them to respond and react in a way which can be done in hours with viable solutions on the table benefitting all the parties in question. Business leaders have been teamed up with IT teams, local teams, and project teams in order to ensure each country, city, and locality has the same policies and procedures in place thereby having a more centralized position in the HR domain and making work easier and streamlined (Jackson, Firtko, & Edenborough, 2007). The brilliant focus that can also be seen as to how HR and the company as a whole must be learning as fast as they are doing, thus making this effective in their overall operating model as well.

Table 12.1 showcases the big reset in HR and how the trends have changed in the HR sphere of work thereby calling them 'resilient HR', abled and empowered to battle any challenging situation.

Shared awareness and studying the ongoing trends and topics have also been included and are considered necessary in order to keep oneself up-to-date with the current happenings and ensure that teams across a country or region are aware about how the teams in the other region operates, thereby

Table 12.1   The Big Reset in HR Today

Responsive (Efficient)	Resilient (Adaptive)
Operating model – centralized control and distributive model of execution	Operating model – distributed control and centralized model of coordination
• HR tech strategies integrated • People analytics • Integrated experiences for recruitment • Strong focus on business priorities	• Client needs at the helm • Teams cross-functional • Flexible and agile pool of people working on different projects • Skills and capabilities tapped well
Nature – Strategic, diverse, inclusive, and experience-oriented	Nature – Collaborative, well-coordinated, cross-trained, and agile
Success – Efficiency and overall employee experience enhanced	Success – Quality and speed of responses increased

making the response time to any situation even more quick and rapid. With this, the top roles of the CHRO or VP of HR have also been redesigned in such a way that they are not only organizers of the HR function now but also a supporter and cheerleaders for the overall work being performed by the HR team. What is imperative here is that the crisis was not just a health crisis but an economic transformation for organizations across the globe who learnt to handle and fight any circumstance of this magnitude in a resilient and determined manner, wherein the people of the organization are assured that they are a part and that if things go haywire, the organizations will ensure that the changed experience is only enhanced for the better and hence, these rapid responsive teams of HR helped greatly achieve this at all levels especially post the crisis (Yu et al., 2022). Resilient HR is not just about HR or the functions that are being performed – it is a way for HR professionals to drive, support, empower, and enable businesses to thrive and survive every business transformation that an organization undergoes.

12.1.4 HRM Practices for Improving Employee Resilience

After an in-depth research on this topic, it has been found that there is less empirical evidence to prove how resilience plays out in a team or individual environment and amongst different situations, however, various HRM practices that can be developed to foster resiliency at the workplace make it intriguing to see how one can build on resilience and build teams which can enhance the overall employee-client, client-organization, or employee-organization relationships (Gottman et al., 1998). The need for innovative HR practices in the field of resilience has arisen to strengthen an employee's overall value and enable them to survive and flourish in a world of challenging times and emerge as a winner.

Various innovative channels that can be built upon in order to mould a more resilient HR are as follows:

i. Transparent communication: A critical aspect, optimum communication channels need to be designed and formed to make employees aware of the changes taking place and significant business-decisions which impact the overall organization (Ilyaz & Shamsi Rizvi, 2021). Thus, this plays a significant role in reducing stress and burnout in the short- and long-run.

ii. Improved positive psychology: Activities which engage employees and shape a positive psychological attitude will eventually help to enhance their overall well-being thereby creating a more resilient workforce.

iii. Enhanced social capital: Essentially meaning the relationships and interactions at the workplace contributing to the development of core ideals and culture at the workplace, the hybrid form of work has altered these and new networking and commitment strategies have to be built upon in order to build a better resilience.

iv. Training: Effective and efficient structuring of work alongside re-evaluating an employee's skill-sets, knowledge and expertise will help to align models of training which will run parallel to enhancement and engagement of employees at the workplace in a more effective manner. These training programs can also be designed in such a way that they are inclusive, diverse, and generate a sense of excitement through which employees are trained in a more positive and stress-free environment.

v. Adaptive work culture: This will inculcate innovative ideas and plans from the workforce themselves in order to create a more resilient organizational culture which will support each one of them on every front and they will learn to adjust and adapt to one another as well in demanding situations.

vi. Stigma-prevention practice: Zero-tolerance policies and a culture which fosters inclusivity at all levels should be prioritized and clearly highlighted across regions thereby reducing internal anxiety issues amongst employees and discussions over trivial matters which will eventually lead to a more resilient workforce, ready to face any situation since they will be able to adapt not only to the surroundings but to each other at a different level.

Human being's general do not know the intensity and coming of any crisis and, hence it is always better to build on various trends and practices for the workforce and being resilient for employees only comes with time, with a proper work-life balance wherein they are capable enough to adapt to situations challenging for them in every sphere. These practices will help any organization to design and formulate creative practices for their employees in order to enhance the resiliency of workforce at a larger scale across regions, with uniform practices in place.

12.2 Conclusion

The topic of resilience has not been in research for long and hence, this chapter with the various sources in place has explored resilience not only from an employee perspective but from an organization point of view as well. In today's era, when organizations are improving at every step of the way with rapid and enhanced technology in place, it is also essential how HR has evolved, in what capacity and what are the various transformations that have come into play since the time of a deadly pandemic the whole world survived. It also throws light upon the practices that organizations can develop to enhance resiliency thereby enable and empower employees to be resilient in the face of any demanding situation. However, a more systematic and in-depth investigation of the factors that have shaped resilience so far and the influences that it undergoes in organizations, by which it influences the workforce at large is critical to be understood at this stage of the world transforming every day.

References

Amir, M. T., & Standen, P. (2019). Growth-focused resilience: development and validation of a new scale. *Management Research Review*, *42*(6), 681–702. https://doi.org/10.1108/MRR-04-2018-0151

Avey, J., Newman, A., & Herbert, K. (2022). Fostering employees' resilience and psychological well-being through an app-based resilience intervention. *Personnel Review*. https://doi.org/10.1108/PR-08-2021-0612

Chakraborty, S., Pandey, S., & Khurana, A. (2023). Psychological contract types influence on innovative work behaviour: mediating role of leader–member exchange in service sector during pandemic. *FIIB Business Review*. https://doi.org/10.1177/23197145231156072

Gottman, J. M., Coan, J., Carrere, S., Swanson, C., Gottman, J. M., Coan, J., Carrere, S., & Swanson, C. (1998). Predicting marital happiness and stability from Newlywed interactions published by : national council on family relations predicting marital happiness and stability from Newlywed interactions. *Journal of Marriage and Family, 60*(1), 5–22. https://doi.org/10.2307/353438

Hartwig, A., Clarke, S., Johnson, S., & Willis, S. (2020). Workplace team resilience: a systematic review and conceptual development. *Organizational Psychology Review, 10*(3–4), 169–200. https://doi.org/10.1177/2041386620919476

Hiebert, B. (2014). *Creating a Resilient Workplace University of Calgary.* January 2006.

Ilyaz, A., & Shamsi Rizvi, Y. (2021). *Innovative HRM Practices for Improving Employee Resilience in the Era of COVID-19.*

Jackson, D., Firtko, A., & Edenborough, M. (2007). Personal resilience as a strategy for surviving and thriving in the face of workplace adversity: a literature review. *Journal of Advanced Nursing, 60*(1), 1–9. https://doi.org/10.1111/j.1365-2648.2007.04412.x

Näswall, K., Malinen, S., Kuntz, J., & Hodliffe, M. (2019). Employee resilience: development and validation of a measure. *Journal of Managerial Psychology, 34*(5), 353–367. https://doi.org/10.1108/JMP-02-2018-0102

Pandey, S., Ruhela, V., & Ruhela, S. (2021). Precursors and ramifications of creativity on innovation in product design teams-a study on Indian information technology sector. *Journal of Physics: Conference Series, 1860*(1), 012014.

Rees, C. S., Breen, L. J., Cusack, L., & Hegney, D. (2015). Understanding individual resilience in the workplace: the international collaboration of workforce resilience model. *Frontiers in Psychology, 6*(FEB), 1–7. https://doi.org/10.3389/fpsyg.2015.00073

Ruhela, V., & Pandey, S., (2022). Emotional Intelligence, Conflict Management Styles and innovative Work Behaviour - A Study on Indian Employees. *International Journal of Early Childhood Special Education, 14*(4), 2678–2684.

Yu, M., Wen, J., Smith, S. M., & Stokes, P. (2022). Building-up resilience and being effective leaders in the workplace: a systematic review and synthesis model. *Leadership and Organization Development Journal, 43*(7), 1098–1117. https://doi.org/10.1108/LODJ-09-2021-0437

Index

Note: Page numbers in *italics* indicate a figure and page numbers in **bold** indicate a table on the corresponding page.

accelerator 2, 89
Accenture 53
adaptive work culture 162
AI *see* artificial intelligence
AI-driven predictive "attrition program" 153
AI enablement strategy 68
algorithm management 61
analytics in business 120
ANOVA 72, **73**
anti-image correlation 72
anxiety 139
applicant tracking systems (ATS) 3
appointment letters 12
article searching process *134*
artificial general intelligence 35
artificial intelligence (AI) 1–2, 13, 17, 19–22,
    99, 118; algorithms 20; behaviour
    control 64; benefits 44; cognitive
    computing 36; in compensation
    and benefits 42–43; computer
    vision 37; as decision-making tool
    20, 64; deep learning 36; devices
    20–21; employee retention approach
    147–153; employees management
    61; evolution 34–35; in HRM 37–38,
    43–45; investment in 35; machine
    learning 35–36; management systems
    63; natural language processing 37;
    outcomes, control of 64; overview 34;
    in performance management 41–42;

recruiting systems 21; in recruitment
    and selection 39–40; in training and
    development 40–41; trust in 64; *see
    also* digitalisation in HR; organization
    performance and AI; robotics in HR
artificial neural networks (ANNs) 148
assisted intelligence 33
ATS *see* applicant tracking systems
augmented HR 151
augmented reality (AR) 96–97
automation 12, 26; in HRM settings 22, 101
autonomous intelligence 33
AWS Blockchain 52

background verification (BGV) 11–12, 102
Beautiful Soup (BS4) 63
Beowulf 52
BeSure 52
Big data 2, 24
blockchain-based cryptocurrencies 118
blockchain-based value creation in HR 119–122
blockchain technology 99, 102, 104–105;
    360-degree feedback 56; accessible
    124; architectures 106; benefits *122*;
    cloud computing, protection of
    105–107; compliance and auditing
    123; contract management solutions
    122; cost-efficient 123; data in
    blocks 51; data protection 109–110;
    decentralized database 123;

digital ledgers 117; efficiency of employee workflows 124; on employee life cycle 52–57; fingerprints and iris scans for attendance 123; in global markets 113–114; history 118–119; and HRM value chain 123–124; infrastructure 105; law and authentication 109–110; managerial implication 125; monitoring surveillance 110–113; network 107; overview 51; in payroll 120; performance management 121; personal data and privacy protection 121; private 106; in recruitment process 120; security, fraud prevention and productivity gains 110; security and privacy 123; technological innovations in HR activities 108–109; training, usage in aligning 56; transactions 51; transparency 124; trust relations and confidentiality 107–108; trustworthy verification 120; uses in HR *54*; value in HRM 122–124
body heat sensor desk hardware 18
brand resonance 99
business: incubators 88–89; intelligence techniques 7; online sales 62; operations 28

Capgemini 28
change readiness 6
Chatbots 4, 39, 150–151; employee's mood analysis 151
cloud computing 2, 105–107
coding 16
coefficient of determination 74; of variable 72, **74**
cognitive computing 36
compensation 119
compliance and auditing 123
computer-based intelligence 62, 66
Computer-generated AI programming sheet 69, *70*
computer vision 37
connected employee 67
contract management 119, 122

COVID-19 pandemic 156; work-from-home culture 118
cryptographic hashing 117
cyber-physical systems 2
cybersecurity 99; risks 121

Dash library 63, 69–71
data analysis 15, 68
data analytics 7
data authenticity 110
data privacy 56
data sharing 56
data usage and protection policies 53
decentralization 105, 117
decentralized autonomous organization (DAO) model 53
decentralized employment system (D-ES) 109
decision-making 19
decision support 28
deep learning (DL) 25, 36, 148
Deloitte 14
digital environment 96
digitalisation in HR 16; advanced technologies 17–19; coding 16–17; intelligence synthesised 19–22; thematic analysis 17
digital learning 139
digital platforms for talent management 85
digital recruitment, investment in 135
diversity and inclusion analytics 8

e-commerce 5, 98
Electrical Engineering (EE) 13
electronic human resource management (eHRM) 17, 24, 26, 100
electronic performance measurement (EPM) 18
electronic recruitment (e-recruitment) 18
emergence, roles in 5
employee: attitude 62; behaviour 63; commitment 62; involvement 65; performance 155
employee engagement 62, 65; analytics 8; employee performance 66–67; levels 67; motivation 65–66; and retention *150*

employee life cycle: blockchain technology on 50–57; stages 52–53
employee retention approach 147–148, 150; AI 148; AI as identifier 151–152; AI-driven training and learning 152; AI to engage, role of 152; augmented human resource 151; career planning 152; Chatbot 151; conflict management, solve 153; employee's mood analysis 151; employee's sentiment pattern analysis 150–151; flight-risk employees 151–152; rate of retention 150; strategic change in human resource management 148–150; succession planning 152–153; talent nourishment 152
employee self-service (ESS) 3–4; software 18
employees management and AI 61
employee verification 119
employment types, shifting 4
ESS *see* employee self-service
Etch 52
eXo platform 52

Facebook (Meta) 97
fingerprints and iris scans for attendance 123
first industrial revolution 1–2
formalization 136
fourth industrial revolution *see* Industry 4.0
freelance: and part-time opportunities 19; workers 81

Gallup 62, 67
Gartner 28, 51, 148
General Data Protection Regulation (GDPR) 25, 121
Generation X 131
Generation Z 129–132, 137, 140
gig economy and HR management 79–80; accelerator 89; challenges to recruiters 86–88; employers' lookout 92–93; flexibility and autonomy 90; flexibility and managing people 91; freelancers in 92; incubators 88–89; lack of standardized job titles 87;

legal implications 80–82; maintaining and promoting HR agility 82–85; policy development for hybrid employee 91–92; revenue diversification 90
gig workers: classification of 80–81; compliance and legal issues 86–87; discrimination and harassment 82; employee benefits 81–82; identifying and attracting 86; jurisdiction's governing regulations 87; labour law compliance 81; lack of standardization 87; managing multiple platforms 88; remote teams, management 87; retention 87; skills and competencies evaluation 86
Gospel Technology 52

Hidden Risks of Recruitment, The (Walker) 110
high data transfer 2
HR agility in gig economy 82–83; culture of agility 84; diversity and inclusion 84–85; feedback culture 85; flexibility of employment 84; flexible workforce 83–84; technology 85
HR in metaverse: automation 101; compliance automation 102; faster learning experience 101; talent acquisition 100; work-life balance 100–101; *see also* metaverse
HRM *see* human resource management
HR procedure in MNCs 11; appointment letters 12; background verification 11–12; paid-in-full employees 12; robotic process automation (RPA) 12
HR transformation and resiliency 156–163; workplace 157–158
human-AI interaction 19
human capital value mapping 6–7
human–computer interaction 4–5, 38, 149
humanoid robots 13
human resource: adaptability 83; agility 83; practices 7; strategies and technological advancement 5–7

human resource information system (HRIS) 38
human resource intelligence (HR intelligence/analytics) 7–9; compliance 9; data-driven decision-making 8–9; efficiency 8; employee experience 9; talent acquisition and management 9
human resource management (HRM) 13, 26, 100; AI software 21; barriers to 44–45; benefits of 43–44; compensation and benefits 42–43; decision-making 21; framework development 22–23; functions 39; managerial implications in 24–25; performance management 41–42; recruitment and selection 39–40; training and development 40–41
human resource strategic management (HRSM) 149
human resource (HR) transformation 158
human-robot cooperation 17
hybrid employee, policy development for 91–92

IBM 148, 153
IBM Garage 52
image processing 99
incubators 88–89
independent contractors *see* gig workers
Industrial Internet of Things 2
Industry 4.0 1; embedding technology 7; importance 2–5
information management (IM) 24
Infosys 11
innovativeness 141
intelligent automation 23–24; business operations and decision support 28; employment opportunities 28; limitations and future research directions 25–27
Internet of Things (IoTs) 2, 99
interoperability 96

job: performance 37; replacement 19, 22; security 21, 82; sharing 84
Job.com 52
JSON format 68

Kaiser–Meyer–Olkin (KMO) test 71
key responsible authorities (KRAs) 101
key result area (KRA) 139
key-value pair format 68

labour law compliance 81
leadership capabilities 6
learning management systems (LMSs) 4
linear regression model 69
LMSs *see* learning management systems
logistic regression 69
Lympo 52

machine learning (ML) 13, 25, 32, 35–36, 148
machine work time, enhanced 4–5
Marketsandmarkets report 54
massive open online courses (MOOCs) 139
material waste 16
Matplotlib 63
mental health 130
Merkle Trees 118
metaverse 95–96; 3D technology 98; brand management 98–99; business interface 98; cyber security 99; digital economy 96–97; in HR 100–102; manufacturing industry 98; mechanism 96; ownership of 97; technology upgradation under integration 99; tools of gamification 99; value creation mechanism 97–98; WEB 3.0 metaverse technology 99–100
microchip wrist implantation 18
millennials 131
motivation to employee 65–66
multinational corporation (MNC) 11

natural language processing (NLP) 36–37, 63, 99
neural technologies (NT) 13
new-generation workplaces **133**
NumPy 63

Oculus Vision Tech. 97
organizational effectiveness 156

organizational factors affecting innovative
HR practices and systems 129–131,
142; managerial implication
140–141; methodology 132–134;
new-generation workplace 135–138;
performance appraisal 139; PRISMA
diagram 134–135; recruitment
138–139; reward and recognition
140; supervisor's feedback/
communication 140; training 139
organizational innovation 135
organizational structure *22*
organization missions 160
organization performance and AI 61–62;
controls for AI employees 63–64;
employee engagement 65–67;
employee performance 66–67;
hypothesis of study 67–68; Pearson
correlation 72; problem statement
62; regression 72–74; reliability 71;
research methodology 68; research
objectives 63; result
69–71; sampling acceptability 71–72

paid-in-full employees 12
Pandas 63
payroll management system *119*
payroll procedure 12
peer-to-peer communication 107
Peoplewave 52
performance management *119*; analytics 8;
software 4
personal data *119*
personal digital assistance 20
Pickle module 63
policy development for hybrid employee
91–92
positive job outlook 5
positive psychology 162
predictive hiring analytics 8
PRISMA diagram 132
private blockchain 106
programme-based algorithms 148
public-private key cryptography 108
Python 63

Q-commerce 98

recruiting 119
recruitment 19, 124, 138–139; process 120
regression 72–74
reliability 71
remote servers 2
remote teams, management 87
Resume Polishers 113
return on investment (ROI) 16
revenue diversification 90
robotic process automation (RPA) 11, 15
robotics in HR 2, 4, 10, 12–14; accuracy
15; cost 15; effectiveness increase
15; future 15; implementation 14;
lean process 16; mass joblessness
16; productive work 15; safe and
simple 15
robots 2, 17; utilisation 13
RPA bot 11–12

sampling acceptability 71–72
scikitlearn 63
second industrial revolution 1–2
Selenium 63
Siri 19
skills and competencies evaluation 86
skills enhancing 5
small- and medium-sized businesses
(SMBs) 110
small private online courses (SPOCs) 139
smart contracts 108
social capital 162
social media interaction 99
social networking sites 105
software bots 14
stigma-prevention practice 162
strategic human resource management
(SHRM) 100, 147
succession planning analytics 8
survey questionnaire 68

talent acquisition 100
technological advancement 6;
steps for robust system 6–7
technological integration 6
technology adaption 4
telecommuting 84
third industrial revolution 1–2

training 19, 162; needs 41; training and
    development 40–41
transparent communication 162
trustworthy system 105
Turing test 34

Uber 63–64

value creation in HR using blockchain
    technology 117–118
Vault platform 52
virtual reality (VR) 96–97

web-based training 20
WebDriver 63

wellness 130
work flexibility 79
workforce transitions 6–7
work-life balance 84, 100–101, 157
work performance 66; counter-efficiency 67;
    participation 67; task execution
    66
World Wide Web (Web 3.0) metaverse
    100
WurkNow 52

YouTube 134

zero-knowledge proofs 121
zero-tolerance policies 162

Printed in the United States
by Baker & Taylor Publisher Services